SELF-MAKING
STUDIO

An Inspirational Doodle Kit
for Self-Discovery and Employability

FAHRI KARAKAS

PUBLISHED BY DIPUBLICA

SELF-MAKING STUDIO

An Inspirational Doodle Kit for Self-Discovery and Employability

Self-Making Studio: An Inspirational Doodle Kit for Self-Discovery and Employability/
Fahri Karakas.
Copyright © Fahri Karakas & DiPublica. All rights reserved.
Published by DiPublica, Norwich, UK.
DiPublica, University of East Anglia, Norwich Business School, Norwich Research Park,
NR4 7TJ, Norwich, Norfolk, UK.
First edition. First published in 2019 by DiPublica.
'Self-Making Studio' Brand is owned by Dr. Fahri Karakas & DiPublica. All rights reserved.

All illustrations and text by Fahri Karakas.
Designer: Murat Simsek
Production Coordinator: Emre Haliloglu

nourish your inner child of

CONTENTS

START ~ POWER ON ~ BE CURIOUS ➡

WELCOME!

Thank you very much for buying a copy of this doodle diary and toolkit.
Nowadays, we witness 'the visual turn': Pictures, images, videos, films, info-graphics, and artwork are more popular than ever. Similarly, companies producing userfriendly visuals from Pixar to Apple, Netflix to Instagram are more profitable than ever. **We live in a golden age of visualization, design, and creativity.**

I have been teaching a course titled "Employability, Creativity, and Personal De-velopment' for a decade. I remember the constant frustration of not being able to find a good textbook accompanying my teaching: *"Why is there no textbook for university students or young people aimed at preparing them for their lives after graduation using visual methods?"* All textbooks on employability seem to be soulless and dreadful not inviting, exciting, or playful. I decided to address this problem through a small contribution: This toolkit that you are hold-ing in your hands or looking at your screen now is my tiny contribution.

In our times, being a young person is pretty scary. There is information overload, accompanied by constant anxiety and stress about an unknown future. There is no job security. We face constant shifts and economic turbulence, along with a perfect storm of technology. There are even signs that Charlie Brooker's Black Mirror dystopia is turning into a reality. We do not know about tomorrow's jobs, workplaces, and organizations. The only thing we can be sure about is the ne-cessity of selfmaking: *We have to constantly learn, be open to change, and disrupt ourselves. We also need to find our own strengths, meanings, and voice in the middle of all the chaos and noise surrounding us.* This toolkit is intended to help you make some progress towards this goal.

I reduce my own anxiety through doodling and diary keeping. I wanted to share my methods with my students and young people out there. The journey of self-making is difficult and complex. I tried to make this journey easier, more engag-ing and memorable using visual tools and doodles. I hope you take the ride with me and enjoy this learning journey.

Dr. Fahri Karakas
November 2019
Norwich, Cambridge, London

About Me:
Dr. Fahri Karakas

★ I am a Senior Lecturer in Business and Leadership at University of East Anglia (UEA).

★ Passionate notebook lover and keeper

★ Serious doodler

★ I work and live across three cities in the UK: Norwich, Cambridge, and London

★ I was born and grew up in Turkey. I did my BA and MBA in Istanbul.

★ I went to Canada for my PhD (Graduation: 2010). I studied and taught at McGill University, Montreal.

★ I worked as Research Fellow at the Open University, UK between 2010-2012.

★ I work as a Visiting Lecturer at University of Cambridge (Pembroke-King's Programme).

★ I am also a Visiting Lecturer at Mountbatten Institute in London.

★ I am an expert on spirituality in management, and I published 30+ articles in leading journals.

★ I am interested in creativity, design thinking, entrepreneurship, and selfmaking.

ABOUT UEA ENTERPRISE FUND

The University of East Anglia (UEA) is one of the top universities in the UK. UEA Enterprise Fund is aimed at producing enterprise activities supporting the university's educational strengths and goals. This toolkit was made possible through the UEA Enterprise Fund.

UEA's motto is "Do Different". How can we help students and young people to find their own paths of 'doing different'? As UEA Chancellor Karen Jones makes it clear: *"We are here as cheerleaders and confidence-givers – giving the support that allows students and faculty to give their best, to have a go, to find their passion and to be the best they can be."*

This enterprise project aim was to develop visual tools and methods – centred on creativity and design thinking - that would help students find inspiration for their careers and lives.

Building on visual methods and materials, I have developed "Self-Making Studio" - a visual toolkit that focuses on visual solutions and inspiring ideas for life design and career design. I aim to develop the art, science, and entrepreneurship of "self-making". I visualise this as my passion over the next decade.

My aspiration is to transform our thinking around 'employability' by shifting the landscape one person at a time: Every student needs to think like an entrepreneur, curator, and designer of their own life. Self-Making Studio inspires and encourages you to play, imagine, learn, create, and design at the speed of life. In your journey, you will experiment with your multiple selves (and life prototypes); borrowing inspiration from diverse realms of life.

THE STORY OF THIS TOOLKIT

In this toolkit I have tried to make a diverse range of developmental and reflective exercises available to my students and the wider audience—individuals interested in exploring and developing themselves and preparing themselves for the job market.

I have been teaching self-making, creativity, design thinking, leadership, employability, and personal development for the last 15 years. Therefore, I have developed a wide range of teaching methods and materials across these topics; most of which are visual.

I have been frequently asked to offer training programmes, seminars, and workshops on these topics. NGOs, multinational companies, schools, universities, trade unions, professional associations, tech communities invite me as a guest speaker or trainer. I have spoken to teachers, entrepreneurs, artists, business people, and students around the world.

There seems to be a worldwide increasing demand for innovative training programmes and toolkits aimed at developing one's capacities for lifetime learning, reflection, sense-making, creativity, and entrepreneurial thinking. This toolkit is developed as a small practical response to such demand. It is aimed at developing what I call 'inspirational capital' - the individual capability for wonder, enchantment, curiosity, learning, self-disruption, creativity and skill development. These capabilities are becoming more and more important in the workplaces of tomorrow. Everyone is expected to keep learning, create value, adapt to changing circumstances, and innovate at the speed of life. The rate of change and innovation has become so scary that we all need personal anchors, principles, and systems in place. This toolkit will help users to develop such personal anchors, principles, and systems.

IN PRAISE OF DIARY KEEPING AND DOODLING

This toolkit is essentially my personal diary. I am inviting you to my personal space. As I think perfection is the enemy of creativity and productivity, you will find that nothing is perfect among these pages. Therefore, you might find oddities, mistakes, or even ugly sketches. All are fine. I encourage you to make similar mistakes. Just start doodling. You do not need drawing skills. Make ugly sketches - it is fine. What matters is capturing your thoughts and ideas.

I have never seen myself as a talented drawer or painter. You will see that the doodles in this kit are not faultless. I try to embrace and sometimes come to like my 'faults'. I think the functional benefits of my doodles (such as engaging the mind, solving problems, visual thinking) are more significant than their artistic value.

My diaries are very precious to me - they capture my plans, passions, emotions, disappointments, and anxieties. I practice what Julia Cameron (the master teacher of creativity) recommends as 'morning pages'. I just write non-stop for 30-40 minutes to capture my stream of consciousness in the morning—it helps tremendously and helps me to focus on what is important ahead of me.

At the heart of this project is my love of personal diary keeping – I have been keeping inspirational diaries for myself and my career since I was 12. I have finished writing countless diaries to inspire myself, to keep learning, to organize goals, to dream big dreams, and to produce ideas.

Recently, I have started to use more visualization and doodles to capture my ideas and inspiration – I cannot stop doodling and I love it. I encourage you to do the same (even if you do not feel that you can draw/doodle beautifully). Doodling will help you integrate and clarify your thinking. You may even end up innovating or inventing new things!

WHO IS THIS TOOLKIT FOR?

Do you need to be a student to use this kit? Not at all – anyone interested in learning, creativity, and personal development could get plenty of inspiration from the sample doodles and exercises.

I have been teaching self-making, creativity, design thinking, leadership, employability, and personal development for the last 15 years. Therefore, I have developed a wide range of teaching methods and materials across these topics; most of which are visual. In this toolkit I have tried to make some of these exercises available to my students and the wider audience—young people interested in exploring and developing themselves and preparing themselves for the job market.

As you will discover, this toolkit will be very useful for also individuals and professionals who are fairly advanced in their careers and lives. Anyone who is interested in getting out of the 'rut' and engaging in a reflective and creative conversation with the 'self' will find this book beneficial and practical. Anyone who is in search of more 'magic' and creativity in their lives and careers will find this journey a good starting point.

After all, we are all seekers, learners, adventurers, entrepreneurs, artists, leaders, and doodlers in our own lives.

Welcome to our journey of inspiration.

HOW TO USE THIS TOOLKIT

Do you need to complete exercises over a specific period of time? No. This kit makes no demands or specifications on who can use it or how to use it.

The purpose of these doodles is to inspire and energize creative parts of ourselves. The final specific goal, of course, could be aimed at developing employability. However, this kit can be used and applied to any aspect of personal and professional development.

A core aim of the toolkit is to encourage you to doodle. Doodling is for everyone and requires no special talent — just find your own style and experiment with it. Doodling will help you in creative self-expression, communicating an idea, inspiring and motivating yourself, reflecting on your own values, and finding your own flow. Through doodling and graphic recording your thoughts, you can be more in touch with your inner compass and creativity, as well as becoming more alive to your senses.

This booklet is a perfect companion for travels — whether by air, bus, or plane. You can use the spaces in between the doodles as creative free spaces to doodle and reflect on your own life and career.

When you go over the doodles, please use them as opportunities for your own self-making: What sense can you make using these drawings as reflective tools? How can you enrich and improve your life?

There is no strict order of these exercises - you can start wherever you want and you can continue in the way that you like it. Your brain actually loves puzzles, play, and imagination. It is a bit like surfing or swimming - immerse yourself and go along with the journey.

Please try to engage in all the exercises as much as you can. Even if you do not feel like you will be able to complete a particular exercise, please challenge yourself to start and try to do just a little of it. If you do not feel like writing, you might try doodling or drawing. If you achieve a sense of progress and momentum, you will be able to complete all or most of the exercises effectively.

ABOUT THE JOURNEY AHEAD

We are living, leading and working in an era of clashing forces, multiple polarities, increasing uncertainty, chaos and change. The collapse of national economic boundaries, rapid technological changes, workforce mobility, cultural diversity, and the increasing interdependence of communities pose new challenges for leaders and organizations. This toolkit is intended to help you discover yourself and prepare yourself for the job market in the light of social, cultural, economic, and organizational changes in the global landscape.

30 SHADES OF GRAY

DOODLE CHALLENGE TO FIGHT BOREDOM

In today's global, rapidly changing knowledge based economy, learning and practicing employability skills is one of the smartest investments you can make for your future. You will soon graduate and work in an ever-changing multinational and multicultural context. So, you have to be independent professionals and lifelong learners. You should get out of your comfort zone, your class, and even your campus/university to become leaders and change agents who have an impact out there.

This is an applied vision and development toolkit; focusing on the development of the new skill sets for future professionals. This kit will increase your awareness and understanding of the changing career context and the employability skills necessary for you. In these pages, you will find several exercises to help you develop and apply employability skills for your career. Doodles are interspersed in between these exercises.

You will embark on a personal journey that will help expand your horizons – if you are ready for applying the exercises here. Exercises are designed to help you think more deeply about your future and yourself: Where do you want to be in five years? What is your dream job? What do you want to achieve? Have you developed the skills and knowledge to differentiate yourself in the job market? What you get from this toolkit depends on what you put into this.

Spend ample time on the exercises. Be engaged and involved. Make this toolkit useful and helpful for your own goals and life. Go beyond the exercises. Start your own diary. Create breakthrough projects and ideas for your future. Sharpen your skills. Challenge yourself. Please make sure you work with your whole body, mind and spirit.

This toolkit will add to the repertoire of future professionals who are bright, passionate, willing to take initiative, care about developing themselves and yet also care about their colleagues, community, and the world. These pages are a wonderful place to start exploring, learning, and reflecting on your career. Welcome to an exciting journey!

SKILLS AND ATTITUDES FOR DOODLING

★ Keep a small notebook and diary with you all the time.

★ Record any emergent ideas or thoughts automatically.

★ Be willing to experiment and make mistakes with doodles.

★ Make time for regular doodling and writing in your diary.

★ Dare yourself to draw quickly and effortlessly without too much planning. Perfection is the enemy - just start.

★ Be willing to share and open up about your inner self and thoughts.

★ Be motivated to make simple doodles even if you have no idea or confidence on how to draw.

★ How can you apply some of these skills and attitudes in your daily life? Please write down your game plan.

YOUR LIFE IS A SPIRAL

MAKE IT A POSITIVE ONE

MY PASSION FOR WRITING NOTES AND KEEPING NOTEBOOKS: A PERSONAL HISTORY

I have been keeping notebooks for the last 25 years to share my dreams and passions.

I have used diaries to put my goals and memories on paper.

I have finished writing more than 250 notebooks over the course of my life. Many of them have been unfortunately lost.

One of the earliest notebooks that I have been able to keep and secure was the notebook that I have used to prepare for the university entrance exams (you can see the cover in the next page).

This was from the year 1996. I was staying in a dormitory in Balikesir, a small city on the Western coast of Turkey. I was studying long hours while I was working to help my dad in the small grocery store in our hometown, Ivrindi (a lovely small town in Balikesir).

I had big ambitions and dreams. I wanted to succeed in the university entrance exam to be admitted into the best universities in Turkey. There were more than a million students entering this exam every year and the competition was intense. Therefore, I needed to solve more than a thousand problems every week. This required great determination. Hence, I started with a motivational letter to myself.

I was coaching myself using this notebook. I designed my own study monthly programmes and gave them inspiring titles (such as 'The Ultimate Mathematics Marathon' or 'Social Studies Super-Hero Supercamp' or 'Hyper. Active Geometry Club'). I incorporated 'play', 'design', and 'story' to my weekly study schedules. I 'branded' each session to make it more playful and invigorating.

The notebook was, of course, 'top secret' - nobody was supposed to see it. I was competing with no one else but myself. I ended up ranking among the top 6 students among 1.5 million in that university entrance exam. Journalists came to my father's shop for an interview asking me the secrets of my success. I responded: 'It is all about keeping notebooks to work, play, learn, improve, and to keep track of yourself and your goals.'

ÖSS ÖYS
HAZIRLIK DEFTERİ

"BÜYÜK BAŞARILAR KOLAY KAZANILMAZ."

FAHRİ KARAKAŞ

OCAK 1996 - HAZİRAN 1996

● Kritik aylar, kritik haftalar, kritik günler, kritik saatler, kritik dakikalar...

Saniyesi altın değerinde 6 aylık bir zaman dilimi. Tik-tak. Büyük finale geri sayım... ÖYS; 3,5 saatlik değil 4 senelik bir yarış. Artık maratonun en önemli son turları.

Atağa kalk. Daha hızlı, daha metotlu, daha programlı. Çözülemeyecek problem, aşılamayacak engel yok. Muhtaç olduğun kudret;

● ALLAH'a olan İMANINDA mevcut.
● İrade ve ders metotunun oluşturduğu gücün karşısında hiçbir set duramaz.
● Sende o azim, bu kararlılık oldukça, hiç kimse seni durduramaz.
● Öyle bir yürekle çalış ki, tasarı yarışı çırak unutma,
— BİSMİLLAH! KAZANMAYA! —

Fast forward to year the 2013. I was teaching in London to 500 students at UEA. I felt rather tired after my teachings were over each day.

I was just watching Turkish TV dramas in the evenings and I searched for an activity that would be refreshing, therapeutic, and playful. I thought—why not doodle? What better way to refresh and re-vitalise myself?

I ended up creating these 54 signs while watching two episodes (Turkish dramas are incredibly long with each episode lasting more than 2 hours).

I loved every minute of creating something new and pursuing an interest.
What could you be working on during your next date with 'your creative self'?

WHAT IS YOUR PROJECT WHEN
YOU HAVE YOUR NEXT DATE WITH YOUR CREATIVE SELF?

Doodle the next page as you like it. Have fun:)

PERIODIC TABLE OF ELEMENTS OF SUCCESS

BY DR. FAHRI KARAKAS

Look at the periodic table and choose which ones are the most critical elements of your success in your current situation. Rank the top 10. Also choose the ten that you seem to have neglected up to now.

Your Top 10

1
2
3
4
5
6
7
8
9
10

Your Neglected Ten

1
2
3
4
5
6
7
8
9
10

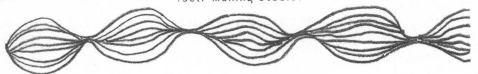

FACING THE ABSOLUTE

Terrifying & Fascinating

EMPTY SPACE

危 机

here and . now

feeling that you can do __anything__ with this page, but you do not know what will come out of it.

You do not know what you will think and feel.

You do not know what is coming or what is emergent.

You do not know what your consciousness means and signifies.

THIS IS YOUR LIFE. NOW. THIS VERY PAGE.

TABULA RASA EXERCISE: FILL THE BLANK SPACE

Our first principle is not being intimidated by the blank page.

Empty space can be refreshing. Empty space is our life — it is up to us on how to fill it (with meaning, dreams, goals, vitality, joy, and passion).

Empty space is freedom. How will you fill it?

EXERCISE: DOODLE YOUR LIFE METAPHORS

Which metaphor(s) or picture(s) would you choose to depict your life?
Doodle it: Experiment and try out options. Is your life represented by a path?
Is it more like climbing a mountain? Is it a caterpillar? Draw as you like.

WHY DOODLING?

You can use doodling and graphic recording in order to:

- Think about the meaning of your life
- Ask yourself questions about your goals, values, and interests
- Discus with yourself: Evaluate your strengths and weaknesses
- Try to work out and solve problems in your life
- Making sense of things, events, and observations around you
- Produce and capture diverse ideas using right brain capabilities
- Plan and dream about future possibilities in your life

STRESS   GUILT   ANXIETY   ANGER   PROCRASTINATION

BOREDOM

LETHARGY

BANALITY

FEAR

tabula
rasa

these pages are your space
for freedom & imagination

nourish & cherish them

embrace your inner creative child

QUITTING   SCEPTICISM   BAD HABITS   LACK OF FOCUS   DISTRACTIONS   SELF DOUBT

FILL THIS PAGE IN AS YOU WISH

Below, you will see the four pillars of this book. If you think of your career as a car, there are four wheels that are important for your career development: Employability, Self-making, Personal Branding, and Creativity. This toolkit will help you discover, learn, and develop skills in each domain.

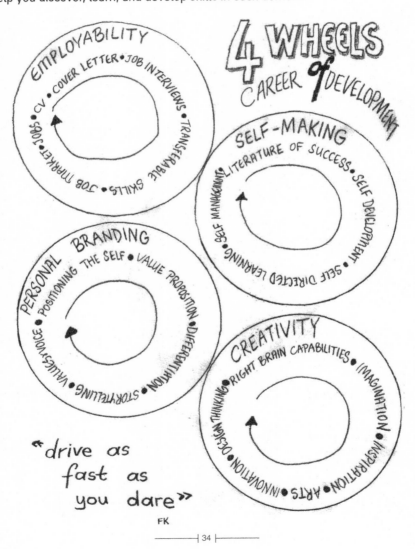

4 WHEELS of CAREER DEVELOPMENT

EMPLOYABILITY — CV • COVER LETTER • JOB INTERVIEWS • TRANSFERABLE SKILLS • JOB MARKET JOBS

SELF-MAKING — LITERATURE OF SUCCESS • SELF DEVELOPMENT • SELF DIRECTED LEARNING • SELF MANAGEMENT

PERSONAL BRANDING — POSITIONING THE SELF • VALUE PROPOSITION • DIFFERENTIATION • STORYTELLING • VALUES/VOICE

CREATIVITY — RIGHT BRAIN CAPABILITIES • IMAGINATION • INSPIRATION • ARTS • INNOVATION • DESIGN THINKING

"drive as fast as you dare"

FK

Self-making is tough. Drawings can be used to bring out fresh possibilities for capturing your imagined future selves. You can doodle or write down your career aspirations, passions, dreams and hopes. Putting them on paper will energize you. Keep a diary to dream, imagine, and capture all your ideas. Start thinking about the elements of your own self-making (example below): Which elements/principles/values are important to you?

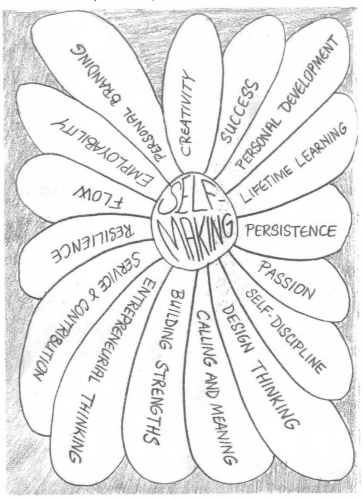

DRAW YOUR OWN FLOWER HERE

EXERCISE: YOUR EXPECTATIONS AND YOUR JOURNEY

What do you hope to accomplish in your journey in this toolkit?
What are your expectations and goals?
Write a letter to yourself that captures these.

SELF-MAKING STUDIO
YOUR JOURNEY STARTS HERE AND
YOU ARE THE HERO OF THIS JOURNEY!

ABOUT THE FLOW OF THIS TOOLKIT:
7 +1 JOURNEYS OF SELF-MAKING

Self-making Studio is organised through eight journeys:

1) Self-marketing: Improving Your Employability
2) Self-awareness: Exploring Yourself and Your Strengths
3) Self-employment: Thinking like an Entrepreneur
4) Self-flourishing: Nurturing your Career Dreams
5) Self-disruption: Learning & Keeping up with the Changing World
6) Self-regulation: Improving your Productivity
7) Self-compassion: Dealing with the Negative
8) Self and the City: A Reflective Personal Journey
9) Which journey(s) do you think will be most beneficial for you?
10) Which journey(s) do you think are most important?

Journey 1
THE PITCH & THE MARKET
Self-Marketing

BOB

I THINK YOU ARE A LOSER AND YOU KNOW IT PRETTY.

WELL GUESS WHAT! I WILL NOT SHUT UP! YOU CANNOT CENSOR ME THERE IS FREEDOM OF SPEECH IN THIS COUNTRY.

ARE YOU TRYING TO SHUT ME UP? MY SPEECH BALLOONS ARE GETTING SMALLER AND SMALLER!!

LET'S SAY YOU DON'T RESPECT ME. WHY NOT RESPECT YOURSELF?

I MEAN WHY ARE YOU DRAWING IF YOU HAVE NO TALENT WHATSOEVER - COME ON.

HELLO GUYS! I AM BOB ON THE GO - YOU CAN CALL ME BOB.

I AM A STUDENT RIGHT NOW, BUT I WILL SOON GRADUATE TO THE JOB MARKET!

IT IS KIND OF EMBARRASSING TO BE DRAWN SO HASTILY. TOTAL LACK OF RESPECT THAT IS.

I AM PRETTY EXCITED ABOUT IT ACTUALLY. I WILL SOON HAVE MY OWN SALARY - ISN'T THAT COOL?

ANYWAY I WILL SEE YOU GUYS AROUND I GUESS. BYE FOR NOW! BY THE WAY - HAVE YOU NOTICED HOW UGLY I AM?! THIS GUY (FAHRI) IS NOT VERY TALENTED, IS HE?! WELL, LET ME SHUT UP BEFORE HE KILLS MY CHARACTER.

IMPROVING YOUR EMPLOYABILITY
THE PITCH AND THE MARKET

In this journey;
- you will be preparing for the job market
- you will be reflecting on your dream job
- you will be working on your CV & cover letter
- you will be role-playing for job interviews

«LUCK IS WHAT HAPPENS WHEN PREPARATION MEETS OPPORTUNITY. »

—SENECA

Meet OBLIVIOUS BOB. He has very few ideas about the realities of job search or the job market.

Meet WISE BOB. He has a better understanding of employability and the job application process.

HI EVERYONE! I AM THE WISER BOB. I LEARNED MY LESSONS THE HARD WAY

AND I WOULD LIKE TO SHARE SOME OF THEM WITH YOU

FIRST OF ALL, THERE ARE SO MANY GRADUATES HAVING DEGREES FROM TOP UNIVERSITIES LIKE UEA

THERE IS A LOT OF COMPETITION FOR GOOD JOBS OUT THERE AND YOU NEED TO FIND STRATEGIES TO DIFFERENTIATE YOURSELF FROM HUNDREDS OF OTHER JOB APPLICANTS.

GOOD GRADES ARE NOT SUFFICIENT FOR SECURING A GOOD JOB. YOU NEED TO DEMONSTRATE RIGOROUS EVIDENCE OF FIT BETWEEN YOUR SKILLS, EXPERIENCES, KNOWLEDGE, AND THE JOB REQUIREMENTS/EXPECTATIONS.

YOU NEED TO SPEND A LOT OF TIME TO REALLY GET TO KNOW YOUR STRENGTHS, WEAKNESSES, PREFERENCES, AND INTERESTS. WHAT DO YOU REALLY WANT TO DO WITH YOUR LIFE? THIS GOES DEEP. YOU NEED TO FIND A JOB THAT YOU LOVE AND FITS YOUR STRENGTHS AND PREFERENCES.

DO NOT CHOOSE WHAT IS POPULAR. CHOOSE WHAT YOU REALLY LOVE AND WHAT FITS YOU. IT IS YOUR LIFE, YOUR CAREER.

YOU NEED TO THINK LIKE AN ENTREPRENEUR ABOUT YOUR CAREER. TAKE INITIATIVE, DO INVESTMENTS, KEEP EXPERIMENTING AND LEARNING, LEARN FROM FAILURE, DEVELOP RESILIENCE, AND CREATE A LOT OF OPTIONS. IT IS ALL UP TO YOU TO DESIGN AND SHAPE YOUR CAREER (AND LIFE)

DID YOU SHOW THAT YOU'VE DONE A LOT OF RESEARCH ON THE COMPANY?

DID YOU WRITE A STRONG AND DETAILED AND CUSTOMISED COVER(ING) LETTER? DID YOU DEMONSTRATE HOW YOU MEET & EXCEED ALL THE JOB REQUIREMENTS?

DID YOU PRESENT RIGOROUS EVIDENCE OF YOUR RELEVANT EXPERIENCES, SKILLS, AND KNOWLEDGE?

HAVE YOU CUSTOMISED YOUR CV FOR THE JOB? IS YOUR CV ORIGINAL/OUTSTANDING?

WHY SHOULD THEY PREFER HIRING YOU INSTEAD OF HUNDREDS OF OTHER JOB APPLICANTS?

WHY ARE YOU A GOOD FIT FOR THIS ROLE AND JOB?

WHY DO YOU WANT TO WORK FOR THEM? WHY IN THIS ROLE?

YOU NEED TO DO A WHOLE LOT OF RESEARCH ABOUT THE COMPANY AND THE ROLE BEFORE YOU PREPARE AND SUBMIT YOUR JOB APPLICATION.

Employability involves a mix of skills, competences, and attitudes required to do any job. Please see the list below. Think of evidence and examples you can demonstrate/share regarding your own employability skills.

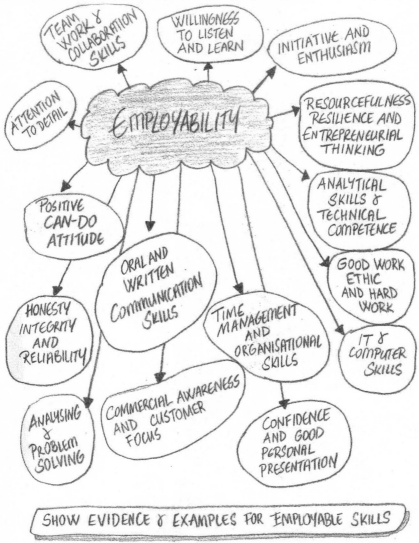

SHOW EVIDENCE & EXAMPLES FOR EMPLOYABLE SKILLS

BRAINSTORM ABOUT YOUR EMPLOYABILITY EVIDENCE BELOW:

What do you think about your employability?

How can you demonstrate evidence on some of the skills and attitudes?

YOUR TOP EMPLOYABLE SKILLS EXERCISE

What are your top 3 employable skills? Choose from the list below:

1) Oral and written communication
2) Team work and collaboration
3) Using initiative and being self motivated
4) Working under pressure
5) Problem solving and creativity
6) Project management
7) Ability to learn and adapt
8) Analytical thinking and numeracy
9) Negotiation and conflict resolution
10) Leadership and
11) Cross-cultural understanding
12) Entrepreneurial thinking

Please come up with your evidence for each of these skills. Think of specific examples/cases for skills you have used. Make your evidence rigorous and specific. Try to incorporate numbers, the context, and your role.

THINK ABOUT YOUR DREAM JOB

Think about your dream job. Visualise and respond:

Which company/organization?

Which department? What is your job title and role?

Which city are you working in?

What is your salary?

Why is this your dream job?

THINK ABOUT YOUR DREAM JOB

How is the organizational culture?

How do you spend your work day?

Which skills and knowledge are you using?

What do you hope to achieve?

Where do you imagine yourself after 5 years? 10 years?

DO RESEARCH AND PREPARATION:
PREPARE YOUR JOBS TABLE

Prepare a table of potential companies and job positions you would like to apply for (include deadlines and requirements).

Analyse the job ad requirements and how you match them. In your application, how will you demonstrate evidence that you match and exceed these requirements?

Do extensive research on each department/company and reflect on why you are a good fit and how you can bring out your best contribution.

I HAVE GOT THE BEST GRADES. WORKED SO HARD FOR MY ACADEMIC STUDIES.

I SHOULD BE ABLE TO GET THE BEST GRADUATE JOBS OUT THERE — I WILL CHOOSE FROM THEM.

SORRY TO BURST YOUR BUBBLE, BOB, BUT, HERE IS THE UGLY TRUTH: YOUR ACADEMIC PERFORMANCE DOES NOT GUARANTEE A GRADUATE JOB. HIGH GRADES WILL HELP YOU BUT WILL NOT ENSURE YOU TO GET A JOB.

TO GET A JOB, YOU NEED TO DEMONSTRATE A PERFECT FIT BETWEEN THE JOB REQUIREMENTS AND YOUR PROFILE AND EXPERIENCES. YOU NEED TO SHOW THAT YOU MEET AND EXCEED THESE REQUIREMENTS WITH YOUR STRONG BACKGROUND & SKILLS.

YOU NEED AN OUTSTANDING CV AND A DISTINCTIVE CUSTOMISED COVER LETTER TO BE CALLED FOR AN INTERVIEW. YOU NEED TO PERFORM REALLY STRONGLY DURING THE JOB INTERVIEW AND PROVE YOUR WORTH AND SHOW WHAT YOU CAN CONTRIBUTE TO THE TABLE.

A MASTER PLAN TO GET AHEAD IN THE GAME + DETAILED EVIDENCE OF FIT + PASSIONATE PROFESSIONALISM + A STRONG PERSONAL BRAND + RARE SET OF SKILLS & EXPERIENCES + A LOT OF HARD WORK AND RESILIENCE + TOLERANCE FOR UNCERTAINTY + CONTINGENCY PLANNING + LUCK + OPTIMISM. QUITE AN EQUATION!

ELEVATOR PITCH EXERCISE

Imagine you have come across your potential employer at the elevator. You will have 1 minute to talk about yourself, and to summarize your career passion, goal, personal brand and experiences.

Think of 2-3 key ideas about yourself you can articulate at the drop of a hat ("elevator pitch on your personal brand").
Write these ideas down (below).

Please practice this pitch in front of a mirror. Present to a trusted friend. Get honest and constructive feedback on your pitch. Revise and improve your pitch as necessary.

WRITE AND UPDATE YOUR CV
Use the checklist below:

☐ Is your CV clear, concise and well written – no longer than 2 pages?

☐ Is your CV clear of any errors in spelling or grammar?

☐ Is the layout well spaced? Is everything neatly aligned?

☐ Is your CV clear, easy to read, appealing to the eye?

☐ Is your CV up-to-date and comprehensive?

☐ Is your CV free of jargon or clichés (i.e. avoid: team player)

☐ Does your CV include name, address, telephone number and email address?

☐ Is there a personal profile or a specific career objective at the start of the CV?

☐ Is your CV tailored enough to a specific job or position?

☐ Does your CV include the key skills and experiences required for the role?

☐ Does your CV include particular experiences and qualifications that are listed in the job advertisement?

☐ Have you listed brief details of academic and/or professional qualifications?

☐ Is work experience in reverse chronological order (i.e. most recent job first)?

☐ Did you highlight your work experience and key achievements in bullet points?

☐ When listing specific achievements and experience, are there 'numbers'?
"Sales have been increased by 25% in three months"

☐ Are there specific skills (IT/languages), with the level of experience (e.g. basic, advanced)?

☐ Have you listed volunteering/part time/internships/extracurricular activities in details?

☐ Have you listed your professional skills clearly with specific evidence, project experience, or examples?

☐ Is there a paragraph about your personal interests and hobbies to give the CV more of a personal feel? Do these hobbies go beyond generic interests? (avoid clichés: 'reading books and travelling')

☐ Is the CV free of any inconsistencies, exaggerations or unsubstantiated claims?

☐ Overall evaluation: Does the CV show the company that the candidate is the best person for the job? Does it clearly highlight the experiences and skills that match the job advert?

sharpen your focus and
live to the point

▶aim for your peak of excellence
▶find your own peak and
climb towards it

do not ever give up hope

celebrate your small victories
slow down, take time to smile and
enjoy time with your loved ones

PREPARE YOUR COVER LETTER
Use the checklist below:

☐ Does the cover letter address a specific person? Is the cover letter detailed enough (delving into the details of relevant experiences, skills, and knowledge)?

☐ Does the cover letter set you apart? Among 100 other applicants, why should they hire you? (Make a list of the top 3 reasons why you are an excellent candidate).

☐ Does the cover letter address this: With the knowledge that you have about the employer, how would you help achieve organizational goals?

☐ Does the cover letter clearly demonstrate how your credentials, experiences and track record would benefit the company?

☐ Does the cover letter clearly review your unique selling points?

☐ Does the cover letter clearly show that you conducted thorough research about this company?

☐ Is there a reference number of the job opening and is there specific job title in the cover letter?

☐ Is the letter addressed to a specific person (e.g., "Dear Ms. Jones")?

☐ Avoid: "Dear Sir/Madam:" or "To Whom it May Concern"

☐ Does the letter grab the reader's attention in the first paragraph?

☐ Does the letter communicate your key strengths at the start?

☐ Does your letter express how you would benefit the employer if you get hired?

☐ Does your letter include examples of the accomplishments (i.e. proven track record)?

☐ Is the content unique? Do not copy text from your CV verbatim.

☐ Does your letter sound genuine? Does it reflect your personality and make you seem likeable?

☐ Is your letter proofread? Is it free of all spelling/grammar/formatting errors?

☐ Does your letter avoid clichés?

☐ Does your letter avoid phrases such as "I feel" or "I believe"?

☐ Is your letter sharply focused? (i.e. no needless detail or ramblings)

☐ Did your cover letter provide an easy way for employers to contact you, such as your phone number and email address?

☐ Does your letter end with a call to action, confidently requesting an interview?

☐ Does your letter thank the reader for their time and consideration?

to keep balance, keep moving
improvizing
working
reading
understanding
writing

Keep calm, carve a pumpkin AND enjoy your life

adventure
thrill
enjoyment

appreciate diversity

bring out your unique talents, strengths, and skills

PREPARE FOR YOUR JOB INTERVIEWS
Do a mock interview with a trusted friend.
Respond to typical job interview questions below:
(Write down your responses)

Tell me about yourself.

Why do you want to work here?

Why should we hire you? Why do you think you are a good candidate?

What is your greatest strength?

What is your biggest weakness?

Give me an example of a difficult situation at work. How did you deal with this situation?

Tell me about an achievement you are proud of.

Where do you see yourself in five years?

recharge your batteries
nourish your hobbies
connect with family and friends
design inspiring spaces
relax, revitalise & refresh YOURSELF
🌳🌳🌳🌳 ©home 🌳🌳🌳🌳

celebrate and enjoy
the season
and its joyful offerings

have a sharp focus & prioritise
block out distractions ruthlessly
set up productivity rituals
move big tasks right away
tackle the hardest stuff first
work when nobody else is

Be humble and wise
Observe and listen
Read and write
Nourish your mind, heart & spirit

USE NETWORKING TO IMPROVE YOUR EMPLOYABILITY
Use the checklist below:

☐ I introduce and present myself clearly.

☐ I prepare for employability week and networking events in order to maximize my opportunities.

☐ I give out business cards that are attractive and reflect my strengths and interests.

☐ I reintroduce myself to people rather than waiting for them to remember me.

☐ I am a member of a professional or community organization and serve on a committee.

☐ I use appropriate and clear messages in emails and social media.

☐ I use LinkedIn to gather information, make connections and find opportunities.

☐ I am an active and careful listener.

prepare surprises for loved ones
be ready for surprises
leave room for serendipity
embrace emergence
go with the flow
swim
improvise

capture and collect
good memories
colourful experiences
remember good friends
Cherish sights, sounds,
tastes, and feelings
travel & learn more
spend time with beloved ones

drink good coffee and
read good books
study think
write
keep going
get up early
learn
enjoy new beginnings

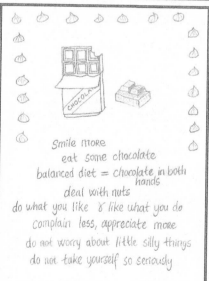

Smile more
eat some chocolate
balanced diet = chocolate in both
hands
deal with nuts
do what you like & like what you do
complain less, appreciate more
do not worry about little silly things
do not take yourself so seriously

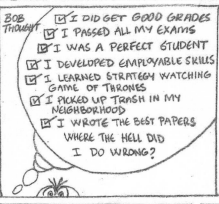

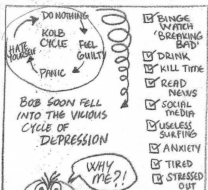

TABLE OF CONCERNS

HOW CAN YOU HELP BOB?
WHERE SHOULD HE START?
IT HAS BEEN 8 MONTHS AND HE IS UNEMPLOYED.
HOW SHOULD HE SPEND HIS DAYS?
WHERE CAN HE GET HELP FROM?
HOW CAN HE REBUILD HIS LIFE?
DEVELOP HOPE & RESILIENCE?
REBOUND?

FK FAHRI KARAKAS

3 Ps IN YOUR JOB APPLICATION PROCESS: PERSISTENCE, PATIENCE, AND PERSEVERANCE

Job applications are tough—there is a lot of uncertainty and stress involved in the process.

Imagine the worst scenario (because this paranoia will empower you). Imagine that you are in Bob's shoes. You could not find a job for 8 months after graduation.

What would you do? How would you cope? What can you do to avoid such a situation? Write down your recovery plan below.

Journey 2
THE MAP & THE INVENTORY
Self-Awareness

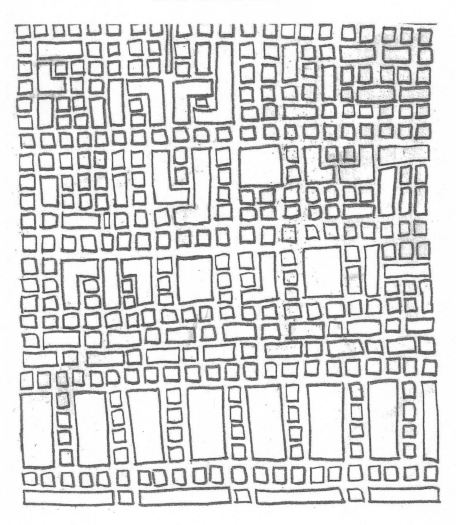

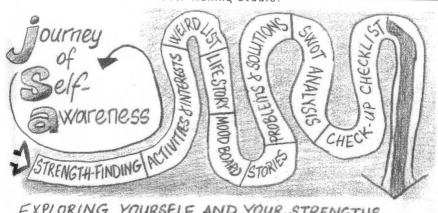

EXPLORING YOURSELF AND YOUR STRENGTHS
THE MAP AND THE INVENTORY

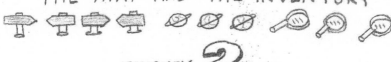

JOURNEY 2

In this journey;
- you will be exploring yourself and your life
- you will be reflecting on your strengths & interests
- you will be reflecting on your life stories
- you will be analysing aspects of your life

《 YOU ATTRACT THE RIGHT THINGS
WHEN YOU HAVE A SENSE OF WHO YOU ARE. 》

—AMY POEHLER

FIND YOUR STRENGTHS

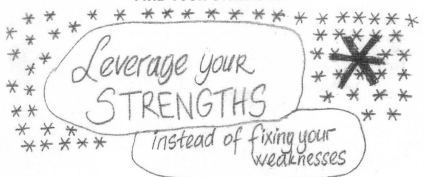

Leverage your STRENGTHS instead of fixing your weaknesses

You do have an amazing unique set of talents, skills, knowledge, interests, passions, and background. There are things that only YOU, can dream of, create, and bring to life. WHAT ARE THOSE THINGS?

Try to find things where you can be THE BEST. Create your own category and build it and be number one in that category in the world. What is that category?

You all have different dreams, hopes, goals, aspirations and passions about your future. You all have different unique gifts, talents, and strengths. If you want to be truly committed and engaged in your career; you need to create your own customized projects based on your strengths and passions. Brainstorm and write down 3 such projects below:

ACTIVITIES THAT YOU LOVE AND CHERISH

What are you good at? What do you love doing?
Create a list of minimum 10 activities or things that represent your passions
and strengths.

I am good at: + I love

* KEEPING DIARY & NOTE TAKING
* DOODLING & VISUALISING
* INSPIRING & MOTIVATING PEOPLE
* OFFERING COACHING & MENTORING
* FOLLOWING & SHARING TRENDS
* TEACHING SKILLS & PERSPECTIVES COURSES
* BRAINSTORMING
* OFFERING CONSTRUCTIVE FEEDBACK
* WRITING & PUBLISHING RESEARCH
* LEARNING ACCROSS FIELDS OF ARTS, BUSINESS, ENTREPRENEURSHIP
* GIVING CAREER ADVICE
* CREATIVITY AND DESIGN THINKING
* DESIGNING IMMERSIVE LEARNING EXPERIENCES
* COOKING GREEN BEANS WITH OLIVE OIL, DILL, GARLIC, TOMATOES
* GENERATING MICRO-STREAMS OF INCOME
* EDITING & PROOFREADING JOB APPLICATION DOCUMENTS
* DESIGNING INEXPENSIVE TRAVEL ITINERARIES
* WATCHING THE SECTOR OF TURKISH TV DRAMAS
* LEARNING & TEACHING ON CREATIVITY & PERSONAL DEVELOPMENT
* GOAL SETTING & SELF-DISCIPLINE
* SELF-MAKING & SUCCESS & INNOVATION LITERATURE
* DREAMING & DAYDREAMING
* USING & STRENGTENING WILLPOWER
* IMAGINING & CREATING
* VISUAL METHODS & TOOLS
* CONCEPTUALISING & CREATING HOLISTIC THEORIES
* CONDUCTING QUALITATIVE & NARRATIVE RESEARCH
* DEVELOPING A GLOBAL MINDSET
* DESIGNING INNOVATIVE CURRICULUM
* SPIRITUALITY AT WORK
* THINKING, LEARNING, & TEACHING ENTREPRENEURSHIP

ACTIVITIES THAT YOU WANT TO TAKE UP AND LEARN

What are the things that you want to learn, improve and get better at?
Create a list of minimum 10 activities or things that represent your areas of learning and development.

I WANT TO LEARN & IMPROVE & GET BETTER AT:

★ DEVELOPING ADVANCED THEORIES
★ DESIGNING & TEACHING WORLD-CLASS COURSES
★ PUBLISHING 4* RESEARCH
★ BECOMING AND THINKING LIKE AN ENTREPRENEUR
★ DEVELOPING VISUAL TOOLS, METHODS & RESEARCH
★ COMBINING MY WORK/JOB & HOBBIES/PASSIONS
★ DEALING WITH ARTICLE REJECTIONS
★ WORKING ON CREATIVE/ARTISTIC PROJECTS
★ DOODLING & GRAPHIC RECORDING
★ TEACHING ARTS, CREATIVITY, & ENTREPRENEURSHIP
★ DESIGNING INSPIRATIONAL VISUAL TOOLS FOR CAREER
★ UNDERSTANDING & USING TECHNOLOGY + TRENDS
★ KEEPING MYSELF UPDATED & AT THE TOP OF THE GAME
★ TEACHING EMPLOYABILITY SKILLS DEVELOPMENT
★ ACADEMIC WRITING & REVISING & REVIEWING
★ SHARING MY WORK & RESEARCH WITH MEDIA & PUBLIC
★ SERVING ON EDITORIAL BOARDS OF JOURNALS
★ SUPERVISING DOCTORAL STUDENTS & THESES
★ CAPTURING THE IMAGINATION OF STUDENTS & PUBLIC
★ CURATING INSPIRATIONAL LEARNING EXPERIENCES
★ ANALYSING & PRESENTING VISUAL DATA
★ CAPTURING CAREER LESSONS & WISDOM OF ROLE MODELS
★ INTENSIVE WRITING & RESEARCH
★ CREATING KNOWLEDGE ON SELF-MAKING
★ WRITING PRACTITIONER-ORIENTED ARTICLES & BLOGS
★ DRAWING HOLISTIC & CREATIVE DOODLES ON SELF-MAKING
★ DEVELOPING VISUAL TOOLS FOR EMPLOYABILITY
★ GAINING FINANCIAL INDEPENDENCE
★ CREATING COMPELLING + CREATIVE OFFERINGS FOR EMPLOYABILITY
★ PREPARING VISUAL BOOK SUMMARIES (DOODLES)
★ DESIGNING EXERCISES FOR PERSONAL DEVELOPMENT
★ INSPIRING CREATIVITY & IMAGINATION
★ LIFE AND CAREER COACHING
★ MAINTAINING SELF-DIRECTED LEARNING & INNOVATION

YOUR 'LOVE' LIST

Create a list of things that you love –

Activities
Hobbies
Realms of life
Pleasures

You can see my list in the next page. Now, please create yours (in the visual format that you would enjoy or prefer).

When do you feel "flow"? How can you combine some of these with your work?

CELEBRATING YOUR OWN 'WEIRDNESS'

Make a list of things that make you "weird".
Do you nourish or restrict these in your daily life?

WEIRDNESS IS WHY WE ADORE OUR FRIENDS.
WEIRDNESS IS WHAT BONDS US TO COLLEAGUES.
WEIRDNESS IS WHAT SETS US APART, GETS US HIRED.
BE YOUR UNAPOLOGETICALLY WEIRD SELF.
IN FACT, BEING WEIRD MAY EVEN FIND YOU
THE ULTIMATE HAPPINESS. ≫

CHRIS SACCA
TOOLS OF TITANS, p. 169.
[BOOK by (TIM FERRISS)]

YOUR TOP 5 WEIRD LIST:

1-

2-

3-

4-

5-

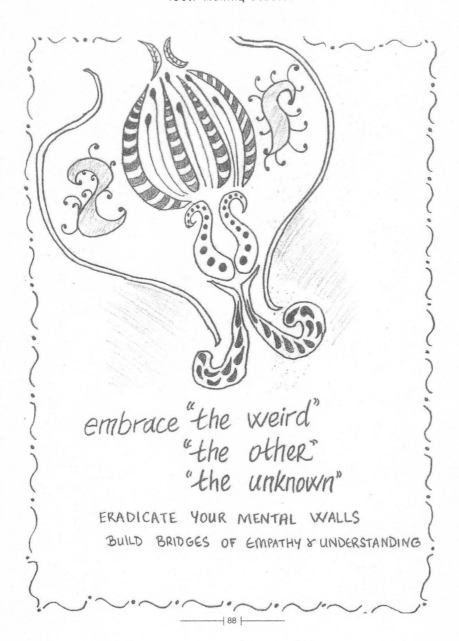

embrace "the weird"
"the other"
"the unknown"

ERADICATE YOUR MENTAL WALLS
BUILD BRIDGES OF EMPATHY & UNDERSTANDING

CREATE YOUR LIFE STORY ON TWITTER
Create hashtags and write them down in the balloons.

YOUR LIFE STORY/BIOGRAPHY

in twitter hashtags

#

#

#

#

#

#

#

#

YOUR FUTURE:

#

#

#

CREATE YOUR MOOD BOARD

A mood board is a collection and arrangement of pictures and text intended to capture your own lifestyle, identity, and dreams.

You can create a mood board physically (cutting images from magazines) or digitally (using Internet sourced images).

Collect images that you like. Think of yourself as a curator and organize these images around themes/meanings or based on what emotions you would like to evoke.

Do not worry about details or perfection. Try to capture an overall feeling or theme based on your interests and passions.

Create the mood board for your inspiration now and put it on your wall.

On the next page, try to create a doodle that resembles or echoes your mood board.

SELECTED STORIES OF MY LIFE

- My parents sold their cattle to allow me and my siblings get good education.
- I got separated from my family at the age of 10 for my education and stayed in difficult conditions of a state dormitory for 7 years.
- I applied for 15 schools for PhD after getting my undergrad degree. I got rejections from all of the programmes and got devastated. I started doing a masters and worked for 45 hours (academic and professional work) to better prepare myself for PhD. Two years later, I got accepted from several PhD programs.
- I had to write four academic quality articles in just 4 days during my PhD comprehensive exam at McGill University. It was the most intense, stressful, and productive period in my life.

WHAT ARE THE DEEPEST STORIES OF YOUR LIFE?

Write down the stories of your life below.

WHAT ARE THE MAJOR **PROBLEMS** IN YOUR LIFE & CAREER **?**

WHAT ARE YOUR **WORRIES?**

YOUR GAPS, MISTAKES & BAD HABITS **?**

WRITE DOWN EVERYTHING THAT PREVENTS YOU IN THE BOX BELOW:

NOW, PLEASE BRAINSTORM AND FIND A LOT OF IDEAS & **SOLUTIONS** FOR ALL THESE PROBLEMS

THINK OF AT LEAST **3** ACTION POINTS FOR EACH PROBLEM

CONSIDER ALL THE RESOURCES NETWORKS SYSTEMS THAT YOU NEED

YOU WILL ACT AS YOUR OWN LIFE & CAREER COACH NOW.
IMAGINE YOU ARE GORDON RAMSEY & YOUR LIFE IS LIKE HIS
'KITCHEN NIGHTMARES' (HOPEFULLY IT IS NOT THAT BAD:)
WRITE DOWN WHAT YOU NEED TO CHANGE IN YOUR LIFE AND CAREER

DO YOUR.. SWOT ANALYSIS ON THIS PAGE

SELF-REFLECTION EXERCISE:

Which movie(s) or TV series inspire you? Why?
Create the script (story) and title of the movie of your life.

CHECK UP CHECKLIST

YOUR LIFE DOMAIN	Your Score	WHAT IS GOING WELL? ♥ YOUR OVERALL COMMENTS & EVALUATION	HOW CAN YOU IMPROVE? ✦ PLAN/ACTIONS TO GO FORWARD
FAMILY/ HOME			
CAREER/ WORK			
HEALTH/ FITNESS			
EDUCATION/ LEARNING			
MONEY/ FINANCES			
LEISURE/ HOBBIES			
LOVE/ RELATIONSHIPS			
TRAVEL/ EXPLORATION			
ARTS/ CREATIVITY			
VALUES/ SPIRITUALITY			
READING/ WRITING			
COMMUNITY/ VOLUNTEERING			
INTIMACY/ SEX			
NATURE/ ENVIRONMENT			
OTHER: (SPECIFY)			
OVERALL			

FAILURES, PROBLEMS, SETBACKS, FEARS:

Go back to each domain in your Check-up + Checklist exercise. Remember your challenges. Remember the cases when you failed or tried something else. What happened? Create a small action point about each domain to go forward.

Journey 3
THE LION & THE SKYROCKET
Self-Employment

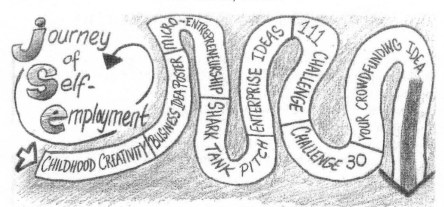

THINKING LIKE AN ENTREPRENEUR
THE LION AND THE SKYROCKET

JOURNEY

In this journey;
- you will be creating entrepreneurial ideas
- you will be thinking like an entrepreneur
- you will be engaged in enterprise challenges
- you will imagine self-employment scenarios

« IF OPPORTUNITY DOESN'T KNOCK, BUILD A DOOR. »
— MILTON BERLE
« ENTREPRENEURSHIP IS ABOUT TURNING WHAT EXCITES YOU IN LIFE
INTO CAPITAL, SO THAT YOU CAN DO MORE OF IT &
MOVE FORWARD WITH IT. »
—RICHARD BRANSON

REMEMBERING YOUR CHILDHOOD CREATIVITY

In this doodle, you can see my reflections and longings about my childhood. Please create your own version of this doodle. It will be on your childhood and your inner child.

What were you really good at when you were a child?

What did you love doing?

How can you develop, nourish, revitalise, (and even pamper) your inner child?

How can you nourish your inner child/creativity at work?

⊛ remember yourself when you were a child.

⊛ you were always playing, drawing, imagining, and creating.

⊛ you drew your logo (above) when you were 13.

⊛ you created & produced the only cartoon/comic magazine at school.

⊛ you created your own TV channels & programming.

⊛ you organized immersive fun events & improvised theatre

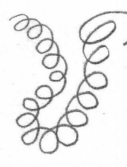

Life is a series of EXPERIMENTS

- WHAT IS THE WORST THAT COULD HAPPEN TO YOU IF YOU ARE AN ENTREPRENEUR AND YOU TAKE RISKS? WHAT IF YOU LOSE IT ALL?

- DO NOT PUT ALL YOUR INVESTMENTS IN ONE BASKET. YOUR CAREER IS ALSO LIKE INVESTMENTS. HAVE CONTINGENCY PLANS. KEEP MULTIPLE OPTIONS. TRY OUT YOUR OPTIONS. SEE IF YOU LOVE THEM. IF NOT, MAKE CHANGES. ACTIVELY DESIGN YOUR CAREER AND YOUR LIFE. ITERATE & IMPROVE.

- FAIL EARLY AND FAIL OFTEN — DEVELOP THE RESILIENCE TO BOUNCE BACK AND LEARN. REBUILD YOUR LIFE

"IF YOU ARE PLANNING TO DO SOMETHING WITH YOUR LIFE, IF YOU HAVE A 10-YEAR PLAN OF HOW TO GET THERE, YOU SHOULD ASK:

WHY CAN'T YOU DO THIS IN 6 MONTHS?"

— PETER THIEL

p. 233 TOOLS OF TITANS by TIM FERRISS

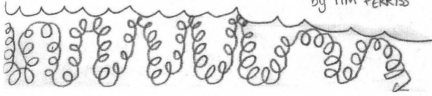

SKETCH A POSTER FOR YOUR BUSINESS IDEA

Below you see my quick sketch that simply outlines my entrepreneurial idea.
Create your own sketches that capture your ideas.

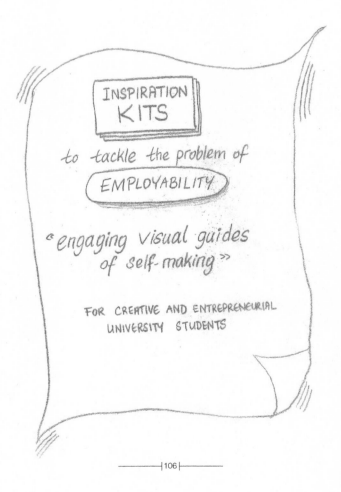

STARTING SMALL: MICRO-ENTREPENEURSHIP

Chris Guillebeau wrote the book titled "The 100$ Start Up" to provide suggestions on creating your own small business.

Patrick J. McGinnis wrote the book titled "The 10% Entrepreneur: Live Your Startup Dream Without Quitting Your Day Job".

Imagine that you have 100 dollars and your weekends to build a business. What would your business be?

Guillebeau, C. (2015). *The $100 Startup: Fire Your Boss, Do What You Love and Work Better To Live More,* Pan.
McGinnis, P. J. (2017). *The 10% Entrepreneur: Live Your Dream Without Quitting Your Day Job,* Portfolio Penguin.

IMAGINE You ARE PITCHING TO SHARKS in SHARK TANK!

BRAINSTORM YOUR BUSINESS IDEAS.
CREATE AT LEAST 30 DIFFERENT IDEAS.
WRITE THEM DOWN.

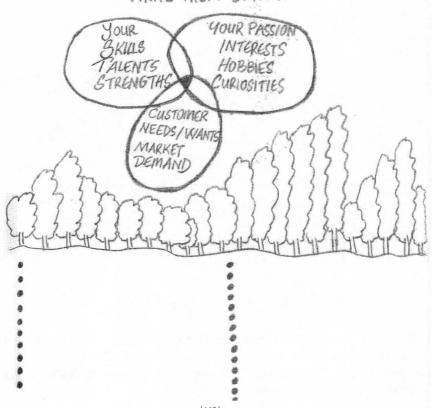

BRAINSTORM YOUR SHARK TANK IDEAS HERE:

Shark Tank or Dragon's Den are TV Shows where entrepreneurs pitch to investors on their business ideas. Watch a few episodes to get some ideas (Many episodes are on YouTube or on Netflix). Imagine that you are going to pitch on one of these shows. Brainstorm and write down your business ideas below.

WATCH (abc)'s

SHARK
TANK

to learn about :

CREATIVITY
ENTREPRENEURSHIP
NEGOTIATION
INNOVATION
INVESTMENTS
RUNNING A BUSINESS
SALES
BOTTOM LINE
MARKETING
PRODUCT DEVELOPMENT
PRESENTATIONS
COMPETITION

YOUR SHARK TANK PITCH:

Choose the most promising and exciting Shark Tank Pitch idea from your list.

Imagine that you are entering the door of Shark Tank. How would you present and pitch your entrepreneurial idea?

(Watch a couple of Shark Tank episodes before completing this exercise to get a sense of the expectations/context as well as the format/structure).

IMPROVE AND PROTOTYPE YOUR ENTERPRISE IDEA HERE

What can you create? Think of product/service ideas.

Think of art or craft work that you can create.

What is the problem that you are addressing?

What is your unique value proposition?

What is your secret sauce?

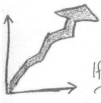

DISRUPT YOURSELF❗

If you have that

BURNING PASSION

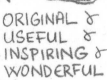

to create something truly ORIGINAL ϭ
USEFUL ϭ
INSPIRING ϭ
WONDERFUL

then, you need to consider

BECOMING AN ENTREPRENEUR

▶ *What is your unique talent and* __unique value proposition__ that only __you__ have?

▶ Which problem are you solving?

▶ Why should people bother to pay for this *offering*? (product, service, or experience, or a mix)

▶ What is your SECRET SAUCE that your competitors are lacking?

▶ How can you keep LEARNING, INNOVATING, CREATING, ADAPTING *at the speed of life*?

CURIOSITY   AWE   FLOW   LOVE

WONDER

PASSION

SPIRITUALITY

COMMITMENT

PERSONAL
DEVELOPMENT

DOING
DIFFERENT

INSPIRATION

PLAYING

CREATIVITY

DESIGN THINKING

STRATEGIC
THINKING

PERSONAL BRANDING

STORY

VISUALIZATION

PROTOTYPING

EXPERIENCE

ENTREPRENEURIAL
THINKING

CAREER

DREAMING

LEARNING

EMPLOYABILITY

ADAPTING

LIFE DESIGN

REDESIGNING

MOTIVATION

self-making

· STUDIO ·

8 MARCH 2017

A BRAND IS BORN TODAY.

YOUR ENTERPRISE POSTER OR INNOVATION SPRINGBOARD

Create your innovation springboard. What is your enterprise idea?

Draw your value proposition below.

Remember that you can combine your entrepreneurial ideas with your role in an organization to add value ('intrapreneurship').

£111! Challenge

YOUR GOAL : To MAKE AN EXTRA £111 EVERY WEEK

Think about at least _20_ different ideas
to help you earn and/or save 111 pounds
every week.

- PART TIME WORK ?
- PROJECTS ?
- GIGS ?
- SELL UNUSED ITEMS?
- USE YOUR STRENGTHS ?
- TALENTS ? SKILLS?
- INVESTING ?
- VALUE CREATION ?
- BAKE SALE ?
- SELL SERVICES ?
- _ _ _ _
- _ _ _ _
- _ _ _ _

- SHARE ECONOMY: airbnb ?
- EDITING ?
- COOK AT HOME ?
- WAYS TO SAVE ?
- SOLVE PROBLEMS ?
- BUY & SELL STUFF ?
- ENTREPRENEURSHIP?
- PRODUCE ARTWORK - ETSY ?
- ONLINE WORK?
- _ _ _ _
- _ _ _ _
- _ _ _ _

good luck!

111 CHALLENGE (FOR PERSONAL FINANCE):
BRAINSTORM YOUR IDEAS FOR EARNING AND SAVING HERE:

FIND SOMETHING TRULY EXCITING, WORTHWHILE, IMPORTANT
AND ONLY YOU CAN OFFER EXCEPTIONAL VALUE AND

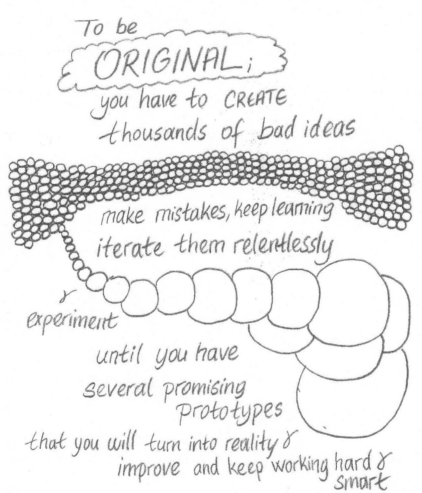

To be
ORIGINAL;
you have to CREATE
thousands of bad ideas

make mistakes, keep learning
iterate them relentlessly
&
experiment
until you have
several promising
prototypes
that you will turn into reality &
improve and keep working hard &
smart

Grant, A. (2017). *Originals: How non-conformists move the world.* Penguin.

CHALLENGE 30:

In his best selling book "The Originals", Professor Adam Grant recommends creating numerous ideas to achieve originality.

Create a lot of ideas to achieve extraordinary success and originality in your career/work project that you choose.

Project Title:
Create 30 ideas here:

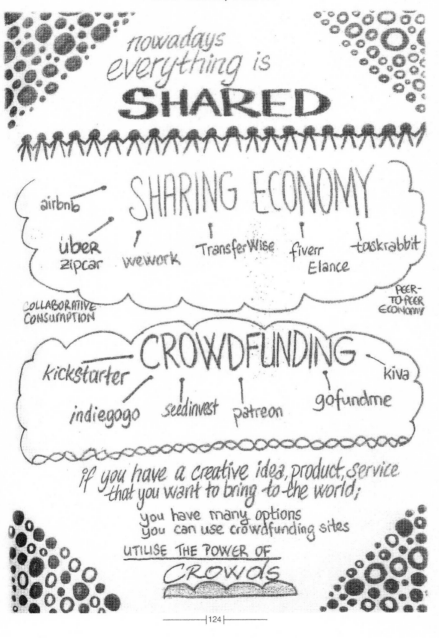

nowadays everything is **SHARED**

SHARING ECONOMY

airbnb
über
zipcar
wework
TransferWise
fiverr
Elance
taskrabbit

COLLABORATIVE CONSUMPTION

PEER-TO-PEER ECONOMY

CROWDFUNDING

kickstarter
indiegogo
seedinvest
patreon
gofundme
kiva

if you have a creative idea, product, service that you want to bring to the world;

you have many options
you can use crowdfunding sites

UTILISE THE POWER OF

CROWds

YOUR CROWDFUNDING IDEA

Think of something that you want to create - something new and innovative (artwork or product). You want to bring it to the world, yet you do not have any money and resources. You want to pitch your idea, and create your own Kickstarter page.

Your funding goal? Deadline? What is your vision? What do you want to create? Any prototypes, samples or videos you can share with your supporters?

Brainstorm your ideas here:

- LIFE IS TOO SHORT FOR CHOOSING A JOB THAT YOU DO NOT LIKE.
- WHEN YOUR CAREER IS YOUR PASSION (OR VICE VERSA), THEN, YOU WILL WORK LIKE CRAZY.
- YOU WILL HAVE SLEEPLESS NIGHTS AND UPS AND DOWNS AND FAILURES.
- YOU WILL MAKE YOUR OWN INSPIRATION. YOU WILL TRY NEW THINGS. YOU WILL CREATE EVERY SINGLE DAY.
- YOU CANNOT PLAN FOR EVERYTHING. THERE WILL BE DISASTERS, MIRACLES, SERENDIPITY, BLACK HOLES, AND BLACK SWANS. THINGS BIGGER THAN YOURSELF AND YOUR WILLPOWER. YOU WILL EMBRACE THE CYCLE OF LIFE AND SWIM WITH THE CURRENTS.
- THE PROCESS OF MAKING ART, CREATING ART IS A BLACK BOX. COMPLETE MYSTERY. BUT PERSPIRATION TRUMPS INSPIRATION. YOU HAVE TO BE THERE, BE PRESENT, AND WORK REALLY HARD. EACH AND EVERY DAY. EVEN IF YOU PRODUCE CRAP OR WRITE GARBAGE. KEEP TRYING. KEEP GOING. BE STRONG THROUGH VULNERABILITY.

THIS IS YOUR LIFE

How will you enrich it and add it more colours, adventure, and spontaneity?
How can you be more flexible and open up to fresh possibilities? And ideas?
Small actions?

Journey 4
THE QUILT & THE EMBROIDERY
Self-Flourishing

people will judge –
not your problem

you are the hero of your life
hang in there – defend your ideas

never give up your DREAMS –

ever!

NURTURING YOUR CAREER DREAMS
THE QUILT AND THE EMBROIDERY

JOURNEY 4

In this journey;
- you will be reflecting on your ideal life
- you will be creating career projects
- you will be reflecting on your values & philosophy
- you will imagine your life's work & contribution

≪ THE TRUE SIGN OF INTELLIGENCE IS NOT KNOWLEDGE
BUT IMAGINATION. ≫

—ALBERT EINSTEIN

FLOWER OF LIFE

As I reflected on the components of a life that is thriving and exciting, I came up with the following flower.

SELF-FLOURISHING EXERCISE

How can you enrich your life? Draw your own flower of life here.

SPECIFIC VISIONS I'D LOVE TO SEE HAPPENING

★ BECOME A PROFESSOR IN MY FIELD
★ GET WORLDWIDE ATTENTION IN MY RESEARCH & WRITING
★ PUBLISH + CREATE VISUAL INSPIRATION KITS
★ PRODUCE + SHARE DOODLE-BASED CREATIVE WORK
★ GAIN EXPERIENCE AS AN ENTREPRENEUR
★ DEVELOP A STRONG PERSONAL BRAND IN SELF-MAKING
★ EXPERIMENT WITH DIVERSE FORMS OF CREATIVITY
★ PRODUCE SIGNIFICANT VOLUMES OF VISUAL ARTWORK
★ PUBLISH A BOOK ON SELF-MAKING & CREATIVITY
★ DEVELOP GENERATIVE SYSTEMS OF INSPIRATIONAL COACHING
★ DEVELOP ACADEMIC ENTREPRENEURSHIP
★ ORGANISE / CURATE AN EXHIBITION OF MY SKETCHES/ARTWORK
★ SHARE IMPACTFUL IDEAS ON MANAGEMENT & BUSINESS
★ OFFER EXECUTIVE TRAINING TO TOP ORGANIZATIONS GLOBALLY
★ CREATE A RICH & INSPIRATIONAL WEB SITE / PORTAL
★ PRODUCE PASSIVE INCOME GENERATING CREATIVE VENTURES
★ CRAFT NEW VISIONS FOR UNIVERSITY STUDENTS
★ SHARE MY PASSION, JOURNEY, LEARNING, VISION WITH THE WORLD
★ DEVELOP SUPPORTIVE MECHANISMS/SYSTEMS FOR YOUNG ACADEMICS
★ CREATE CUTTING EDGE SCIENCE & RESEARCH & KNOWLEDGE
★ CREATE CREATIVE EDUCATIONAL / LEARNING MATERIALS
★ TRAVEL AT LEAST 30 NEW COUNTRIES IN THE WORLD
★ DEVELOP A COMMUNITY OF CREATIVE / VISUAL LEARNERS
★ WORK WITH LEADING ENTREPRENEURS & FIRMS GLOBALLY
★ ACHIEVE CREATIVE CROSS-POLLINATION AMONG MY INTERESTS
★ DEVELOP EXPERTISE ON SELF-MAKING & LIFE DESIGN
★ BECOME A TREND WATCHER & EXPERT ON TV, MEDIA, CULTURE, ARTS
★ EXPERIMENT WITH ELEGANT DESIGN TOOLS & SKETCHES/MULTIMEDIA
★ CRAFTING AND CHAMPIONING PIONEERING ARTWORK
★ COMBINING UNLIKELY DOMAINS & FIELDS CREATIVELY
★ CAPTURING GLOBAL IMAGINATION THROUGH DOODLES

PROJECTS THAT YOU WANT TO REALISE

What are your wishes in your life and career?

Create a list of a minimum of 10 wishes, projects, goals, desires, and visions that belong to you.

1

2

3

4

5

6

7

8

9

10

This exercise has been adapted from the wonderful book of Jim Krause: "D30 - Exercises for Designers: Thirty Days of Creative Design Exercises".

IN PRAISE OF DREAMS

DREAMING, LIKE FLYING,

IS AN ART & SKILL THAT CAN BE
NURTURED IN OURSELVES.
HOWEVER, IT IS FRAGILE LIKE A BIRD
AND BOUNDED BY THE IRON CAGE
(NEGATIVE VOICES & CRITICISM
                    INCLUDING OUR OWN)
DREAMS ARE POWERFUL
    BECAUSE THEY ARE BOUNDLESS
(FREE OF GRAVITY) –
THEY EMBODY OUR CREATIVE SPIRITS
AND BEST TALENTS AND IMAGINATION
AND FREEDOM.

Let yourself to dream big dreams.

Create more space & freedom for dreams

DREAM AND DESIGN YOUR TOP CAREER PROJECTS

Among all your projects, choose the top 3 career projects that you want to bring to life and develop in the following months.

Think of possible titles for your career projects.

Do brainstorming and jot down your ideas in ways that inspire you.

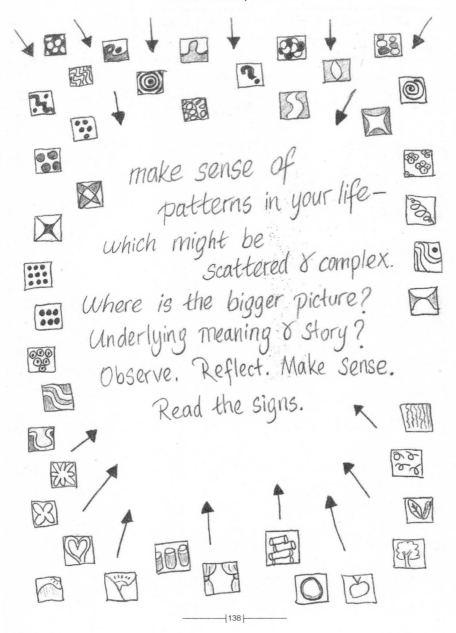

make sense of
patterns in your life—
which might be
    scattered & complex.
Where is the bigger picture?
Underlying meaning & story?
Observe. Reflect. Make sense.
    Read the signs.

THE MEANING OF YOUR LIFE

Write about the meaning and philosophy of your life here.

What is your story? Where do you come from? Where are you headed?

Think of your values and principles that are indispensable. What are they?

WHAT ARE THE ELEMENTS OF THE LIFE THAT YOU LOVE AND DREAM OF AND ASPIRE TO?

You CAN INCLUDE TITLES OF YOUR CAREER PROJECTS, TRAVEL TO YOUR DREAM CITIES, CREATIVE HOBBIES, WRITING ACTIVITIES, ENTERPRISE/VENTURES, JOBS

DREAM TEAM: (COLLEAGUES, MENTORS)		DREAM JOB:	
	DREAM HOLIDAY:		DREAM CITY:
YOUR PASSION PROJECT:		YOUR ENTERPRISE:	
	YOUR HOBBY AS A PARALLEL CAREER:		YOUR WRITING PROJECT:
YOUR LEARNING PURSUIT: (EDUCATIONAL)		YOUR ARTISTIC PROJECT: (CREATIVE)	
⊛ feel free to fill empty cells as you wish ☺	⊛ you can draw, doodle or write anything :)	⊛ include diverse ideas/projects to enrich your life & career	⊛ SKY IS THE LIMIT & DREAM!

REFLECT ON YOUR IDEAL LIFE HERE (WRITE OR VISUALISE):

WRITE DOWN YOUR FUTURE CONTRIBUTION

WRITE DOWN THAT NEWS/STORY BELOW:

WRITE DOWN YOUR OBITUARY

morning ramblings

WHY DO WE LIVE?

WHAT IS THE MEANING OF ALL THIS?

HOW DO I LEAVE LEGACY?

WHAT WILL BE MY MARK/CONTRIBUTION IN THIS WORLD?

WHAT IS MY PERSPECTIVE IN LIFE?

HOW CAN I SUMMARISE MY LIFE PHILOSOPHY?

WHAT ARE MY INDISPENSIBLE VALUES?

WHY ARE THEY CRITICAL? HOW DO THEY MAKE A DIFFERENCE?

EXERCISE:
WRITE DOWN YOUR OWN OBITUARY.

EXERCISE ON YOUR LIFE SEGMENTS

The British Documentary "Up" was initiated in 1964 and interviewed children aged 7 about their lives and dreams. These children were tracked and interviewed again when they were 14, 21, 28, 35, 42, 49, and 56.

Divide your life into 7-year segments and draw the phases based on these years.

1-7
8-14
15-21
22-28
29-35
36-42
43-49
50-56
57-63
64-70
71-77
78-84
85-91
92 -98

1. Draw the segments like a lifeline or a path.
2. Give a title to each segment.
3. What were the major life events or milestones during these years?
4. Think of places/cities/people significant during this segment.
5. Write down your major roles/jobs/projects and key institutions during this segment.
6. At what junction are you at currently?
7. Where will you be heading next? Brainstorm possibilities and write down your dreams.

WRITE DOWN OR DRAW YOUR SEGMENTS HERE:

▷ WHAT ARE YOU CUT OUT FOR ?

▷ WHERE IS YOUR DESTINY ?

▷ GIVE YOURSELF ONE HOUR EVERY DAY TO EXPLORE.
▷ DISCOVER POSSIBILITIES.

▷ DO FIELD RESEARCH. INTERVIEW PEOPLE WHO HAVE
  BEEN WORKING IN INTERESTING CAREERS.
▷ READ MORE. DEVELOP COMPETENCES AND
  KNOWLEDGE.

▷ CREATE PROTOTYPES & MULTIPLE PATHWAYS.
  EXPERIMENT WITH THEM.

▷ KEEP LEARNING EVERY DAY. CHALLENGE
  YOURSELF. SHARPEN SKILLS.

▷ MAKE MISTAKES. FAIL EARLY AND OFTEN.
  DEVELOP RESILIENCE. TAKE RISKS.
  IMPROVISE.

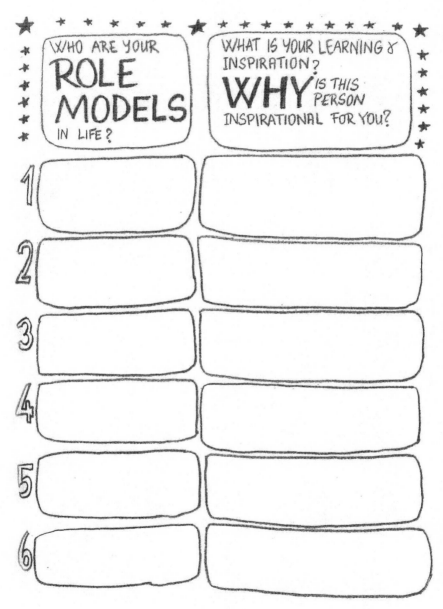

WHO ARE YOUR **ROLE MODELS** IN LIFE?

WHAT IS YOUR LEARNING & INSPIRATION? **WHY** IS THIS PERSON INSPIRATIONAL FOR YOU?

1

2

3

4

5

6

1 READ A BOOK
2 VISIT A NEW CITY
3 SEE A PLAY
4 DEVELOP A SKILL
5 GO TO A BLOCKBUSTER

6 DONATE TO A CHARITY
7 GO TO A CONCERT
8 FINISH AN ONLINE COURSE
9 DECORATE PERSONALISE YOUR SPACE
10 SEE A NEW COUNTRY

11 FIND A NEW HOBBY
12 COOK A NEW DISH
13 VISIT THE WILDERNESS
14 INVITE FRIENDS TO YOUR HOME
15 MEDITATE RELAX AT SPA

16 BUY A NEW MAGAZINE
17 ATTEND AN INSPIRING TALK
18 DO A WRITING CAMP
19 START KEEPING A DIARY
20 DO EXERCISE REGULARLY

21 START A 30-DAY CHALLENGE - SET A GOAL
22 DE-CLUTTER YOUR HOUSE
23 KEEP MORNING PAGES
24 START SAVING & INVESTING
25 CREATE A SCRAPBOOK

26 TAKE GREAT PICTURES
27 SWIM
28 COLLECT EPHEMERA TO CREATE ARTS
29 DEVELOP A PROJECT
30 FIND AN ENTREPRENEURIAL IDEA & APPLY IT

ENRICH YOUR LIFE ONE MONTH A TIME

ADD SOME SPICE TO YOUR LIFE!

AIM FOR TRANQUILITY CREATIVITY PRODUCTIVITY

PREPARE YOUR TED TALK AND INSPIRE THE WORLD!

Imagine that you are invited to present at TED Conference or at the Davos Economic Forum. Prepare a 5 minute presentation on a topic you are passionate about. Express yourself and your breakthrough idea to the world.

LEARNING FROM INSPIRATIONAL CAREERS

From Elon Musk to Meryl Streep, we can learn a lot from contemporary creatives or leaders. What were their dreams and passions? How did they pursue them? How did they make outstanding contributions in their respective fields? From physics to haute cuisine, you can explore the literature of career success through the lenses of dreams, passions, creativity, and selfmaking.

Listen to five BBC 4 Desert Island Discs episodes (choose 5) to explore and learn about careers and stories of inspirational people. Summarise your learning in 5 bullet points below.

1

2

3

4

5

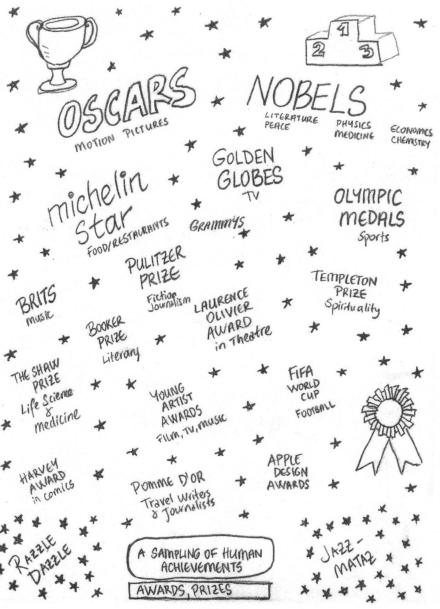

OSCARS
MOTION PICTURES

NOBELS
LITERATURE
PEACE
PHYSICS
MEDICINE
ECONOMICS
CHEMISTRY

GOLDEN GLOBES
TV

michelin star
FOOD/RESTAURANTS

GRAMMYS

OLYMPIC MEDALS
Sports

PULITZER PRIZE
Fiction
Journalism

BRITS
music

LAURENCE OLIVIER AWARD
in Theatre

TEMPLETON PRIZE
Spirituality

BOOKER PRIZE
Literary

THE SHAW PRIZE
Life Science & medicine

YOUNG ARTIST AWARDS
Film, TV, music

FIFA WORLD CUP
FOOTBALL

HARVEY AWARD
in comics

POMME D'OR
Travel Writers & Journalists

APPLE DESIGN AWARDS

RAZZLE DAZZLE

A SAMPLING OF HUMAN ACHIEVEMENTS

AWARDS, PRIZES

JAZZ-MATAZ

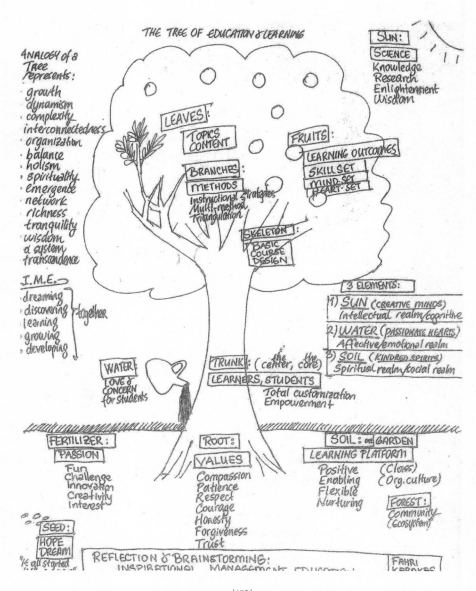

THE TREE OF EDUCATION & LEARNING

SUN:
SCIENCE
Knowledge
Research
Enlightenment
Wisdom

ANALOGY of a
TREE
represents:
· growth
· dynamism
· complexity
· interconnectedness
· organization
· balance
· holism
· spirituality
· emergence
· network
· richness
· tranquility
· wisdom
· a system
· transcendence

LEAVES:
TOPICS
CONTENT

FRUITS:
LEARNING OUTCOMES
SKILLSET
MIND-SET
HEART-SET

BRANCHES:
METHODS
Instructional strategies
Multi-method
Triangulation

SKELETON:
BASIC
COURSE
DESIGN

I.M.E.
· dreaming
· discovering   } together
· learning
· growing
· developing

3 ELEMENTS:
1) SUN (CREATIVE MINDS)
Intellectual realm/cognitive
2) WATER (PASSIONATE HEARTS)
Affective/emotional realm
3) SOIL (KINDRED SPIRITS)
Spiritual realm/social realm

WATER
LOVE &
CONCERN
for students

TRUNK: (the center, the core)
LEARNERS, STUDENTS
Total customization
Empowerment

FERTILIZER:
PASSION
Fun
Challenge
Innovation
Creativity
Interest

ROOT:
VALUES
Compassion
Patience
Respect
Courage
Honesty
Forgiveness
Trust

SOIL: or GARDEN
LEARNING PLATFORM
Positive   (Class)
Enabling   (Org. culture)
Flexible
Nurturing

FOREST:
Community
(Ecosystem)

SEED:
HOPE
DREAM
"It all started

REFLECTION & BRAINSTORMING:
INSPIRATIONAL MANAGEMENT EDUCATION

FAHRI
KARAKAS

DRAW YOUR OWN CONCEPT MAP:
HOW DO YOU SEE YOUR PROFESSION?

This concept map outlines my career/job philosophy utilising a number of metaphors.

Draw/design your own professional philosophy here in the form of a concept map. Feel free to use sketches and metaphors.

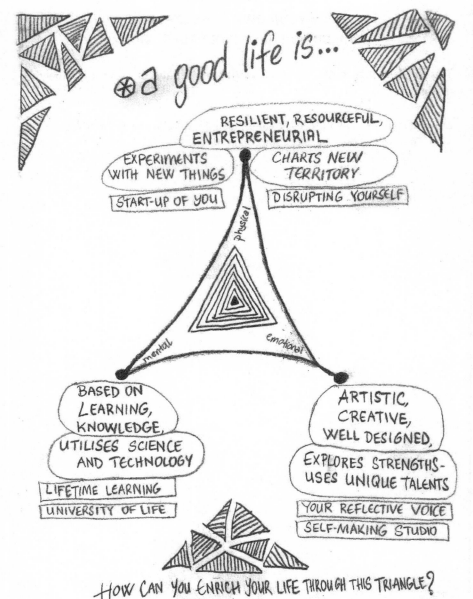

⊛a good life is...

RESILIENT, RESOURCEFUL, ENTREPRENEURIAL

EXPERIMENTS WITH NEW THINGS

CHARTS NEW TERRITORY

START-UP OF YOU

DISRUPTING YOURSELF

physical

mental

emotional

BASED ON LEARNING, KNOWLEDGE, UTILISES SCIENCE AND TECHNOLOGY

LIFETIME LEARNING

UNIVERSITY OF LIFE

ARTISTIC, CREATIVE, WELL DESIGNED,

EXPLORES STRENGTHS- USES UNIQUE TALENTS

YOUR REFLECTIVE VOICE

SELF-MAKING STUDIO

HOW CAN YOU ENRICH YOUR LIFE THROUGH THIS TRIANGLE?

BRIDGING ARTS, SCIENCE & ENTREPRENEURSHIP

Identify and write down some practical action points to enrich your life through bridging and nurturing these three domains:

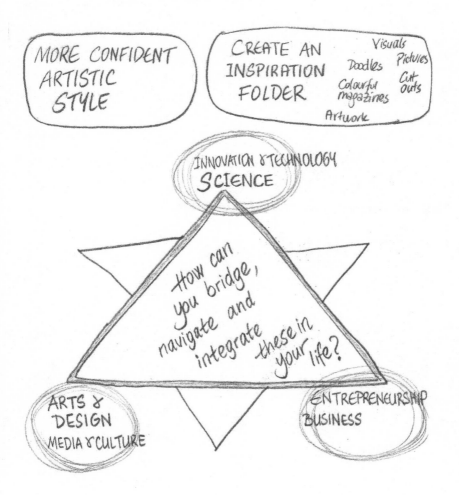

Ideas on fostering your entrepreneurial life:

Ideas on designing your creative/artistic life:

Ideas on crafting a life of learning and knowledge:

Combine your ideas here:

Journey 5
THE BUTTERFLY & THE CHAOS
Self-Disruption

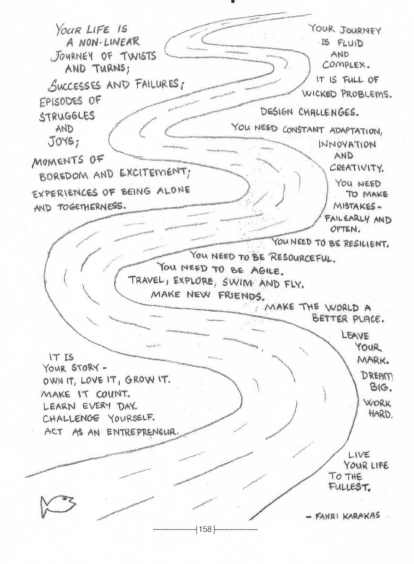

YOUR LIFE IS A NON-LINEAR JOURNEY OF TWISTS AND TURNS;

SUCCESSES AND FAILURES; EPISODES OF STRUGGLES AND JOYS;

MOMENTS OF BOREDOM AND EXCITEMENT;

EXPERIENCES OF BEING ALONE AND TOGETHERNESS.

YOUR JOURNEY IS FLUID AND COMPLEX.

IT IS FULL OF WICKED PROBLEMS.

DESIGN CHALLENGES.

YOU NEED CONSTANT ADAPTATION, INNOVATION AND CREATIVITY.

YOU NEED TO MAKE MISTAKES - FAIL EARLY AND OFTEN.

YOU NEED TO BE RESILIENT.

YOU NEED TO BE RESOURCEFUL.

YOU NEED TO BE AGILE.

TRAVEL, EXPLORE, SWIM AND FLY.

MAKE NEW FRIENDS.

MAKE THE WORLD A BETTER PLACE.

LEAVE YOUR MARK.

DREAM BIG.

WORK HARD.

IT IS YOUR STORY - OWN IT, LOVE IT, GROW IT. MAKE IT COUNT. LEARN EVERY DAY. CHALLENGE YOURSELF. ACT AS AN ENTREPRENEUR.

LIVE YOUR LIFE TO THE FULLEST.

— FAHRI KARAKAS

Journey of Self-disruption

PARADIGM SHIFTS · TECHNOLOGY & DISRUPTION · DESIGN THINKING/GLOBAL VISION · LEARNING · EXECUTIVE BOOK CLUB · PANARCHY · INNOVATIVE THINKING

LEARNING AND KEEPING UP WITH THE WORLD
THE BUTTERFLY AND THE CHAOS

JOURNEY 5

In this journey;
• you will be learning about technology & change
• you will review global perspectives & vision
• you will take initiative for your learning
• you will expand your knowledge & repertoire

《 WE ARE CURRENTLY PREPARING STUDENTS FOR JOBS THAT DON'T
EXIST YET, USING TECHNOLOGIES THAT HAVEN'T BEEN INVENTED,
IN ORDER TO SOLVE PROBLEMS WE DON'T EVEN KNOW ARE PROBLEMS YET. 》
— SHIFT HAPPENS VIDEOS

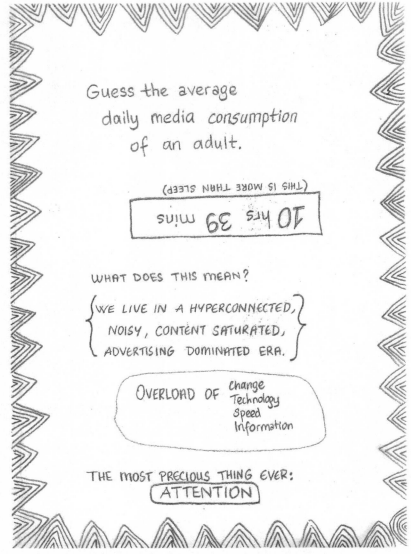

Guess the average
daily media consumption
of an adult.

(THIS IS MORE THAN SLEEP)

10 hrs 39 mins

WHAT DOES THIS MEAN?

{ WE LIVE IN A HYPERCONNECTED,
NOISY, CONTENT SATURATED,
ADVERTISING DOMINATED ERA. }

OVERLOAD OF Change
Technology
Speed
Information

THE MOST PRECIOUS THING EVER:
ATTENTION

Nielsen Total Audience Report, 2016, states adults in the US devote 10 hours 39 minutes each day to consuming media (tablets, smartphones, PCs, multimedia devices, video games, radios, DVDs, DVRs and TVs).

≫ LOVEMARKS & BRANDS

★ CREATE & CURATE

WONDER, AWE, ENCHANTMENT,
SURPRISE, HUMOUR, ADVENTURE

through

STORYTELLING & STORYDOING

that is rooted in
humanity ★

Fjord 2017 Trends Report by Accenture states we witness a shift from storytelling to storydoing. Brands create and enact their own stories by 'storydoing' rather than just 'storytelling'.

The future belongs to...

CREATORS   EMPHATHISERS

ENTREPRENEURS

PATTERN RECOGNIZERS

MEANING MAKERS

STORYTELLERS

ARTISTS   DESIGNERS

INVENTORS

BIG PICTURE THINKERS

BRAND BUILDERS

CREATIVES

CAREGIVERS   CONSOLERS

CURATORS   EXPERIENCE DESIGNERS

ARTISANS   WRITERS

IMAGINEERS   DREAMERS

INNOVATORS

A WHOLE NEW MIND
DANIEL PINK

Pink, D. H. (2006). *A whole new mind: Why right-brainers will rule the future.* Penguin.

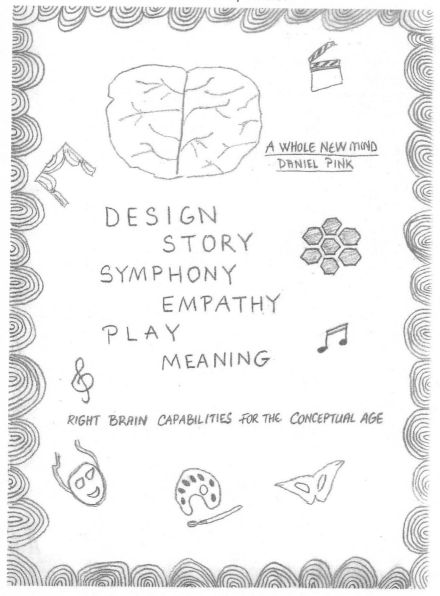

A WHOLE NEW MIND
DANIEL PINK

DESIGN
STORY
SYMPHONY
EMPATHY
PLAY
MEANING

RIGHT BRAIN CAPABILITIES FOR THE CONCEPTUAL AGE

Pink, D. H. (2006). *A whole new mind: Why right-brainers will rule the future.* Penguin.

THE FUTURE, THE TECHNOLOGY, AND YOUR CAREER

Dell report claims 85% of jobs that will exist in 2030 haven't been invented yet.

Technology is disruptive and it keeps transforming workplaces, business practices, and work processes.

How will you disrupt yourself to be prepared for such an uncertain future?

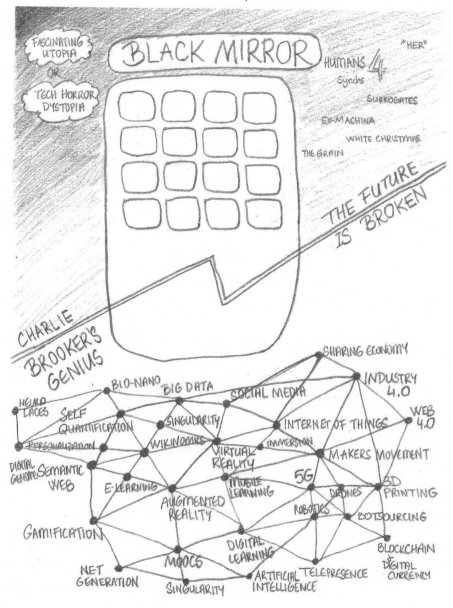

A.I. is already here!

GOOGLE DEEPMIND'S PROGRAMS are

- intelligent
- freaky
- creative
- adaptive
- scary
- uncanny

ALPHAGO

beats master LEE SEDOL

ALPHAZERO

beats Stockfish — (which embodies centuries of human + decades of comp. power wisdom)

4 HOURS after learning the rules of chess

---

2 OPTIONS

FEAR

Freaking out
Fear of missing out
Being alienated
Being stressed out
Fear of the unknown
Fear of unemployment
Fear of change
Fear of being redundant
Existential crisis
Being scared of
      humanity's future
Vulnerability
Surviving as a human
   in the age of algorithms

HOPE

Bewilderment
Adaptive learning
Curiosity
Problem solving
Mental stamina
Emotional stamina
Resilience
Reflection & sensemaking
Cognitive flexibility
Retraining
Self-making
Adapting to change
Experimentation
Imagination
Thriving in the age of
   algorithms

HOW WILL YOU TAKE CARE OF YOUR CAREER AND LEARNING AND SKILL DEVELOPMENT in the age of artificial intelligence?

ACTION POINTS:

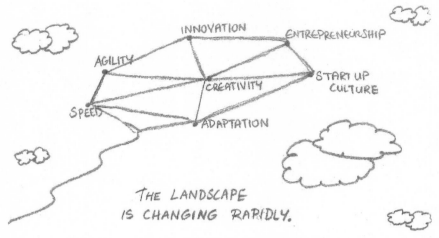

INNOVATION   ENTREPRENEURSHIP
AGILITY
       CREATIVITY   START UP
                     CULTURE
SPEED
       ADAPTATION

THE LANDSCAPE
IS CHANGING RAPIDLY.

THE FUTURE OF BUSINESS LIES IN
CULTURES OF CONSTANT CHANGE, CONTINUAL
ITERATION, DESIGN THINKING AND IMAGINATION.

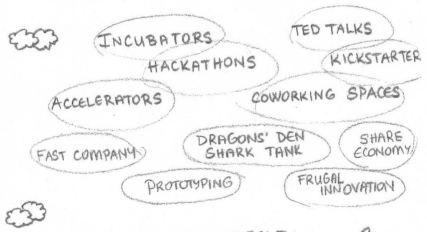

INCUBATORS   TED TALKS
   HACKATHONS   KICKSTARTER
ACCELERATORS   COWORKING SPACES
FAST COMPANY   DRAGONS' DEN   SHARE
                SHARK TANK   ECONOMY
     PROTOTYPING   FRUGAL
                     INNOVATION

DISRUPT & HACK YOURSELF
   REDESIGN YOUR LIFE !

DESIGN THINKING EXERCISE

You are the younger generation and heir of a traditional family business. Your company produces and sells umbrellas.

The sales have recently dropped and the company needs to come up with innovations in this product line in order to survive.

Your task is to use design thinking principles, methods, and prac-tices to come up with a new conception of an umbrella.

Think about both form and functionality of an umbrella: Why and how do we use it? How can you innovate in this product line?

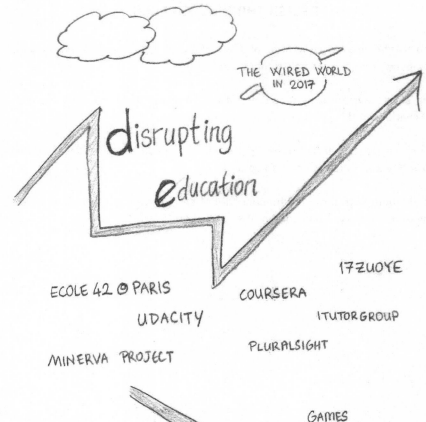

THE WIRED WORLD IN 2017

disrupting
education

17 ZUOYE

ECOLE 42 @ PARIS

COURSERA

UDACITY

ITUTORGROUP

PLURALSIGHT

MINERVA PROJECT

no teacher
no lecture
no syllabus
no exam
no memorization
no fees
no physical campus

GAMES
VIRTUAL NETWORKS
SINGULARITY
SENSE-MAKING
NOVELTY - ADAPTIVITY
TRANSDISCIPLINARITY
DESIGN MINDSET
LIFELONG LEARNING
IMAGINATION

DISRUPTING YOUR OWN EDUCATION

Learning from textbooks will never be sufficient for your career. Much of your learning needs to come from other sources. You need to assume full responsibility and take initiative for your own learning.

Internet, books, blogs, social media, films, TV, games, friends, networks, conferences, museums can all be great sources for your learning, creativity, and development.

How can you make sure you are learning from diverse sources?

What have you learned recently that excites you? How can you increase such learning in your life?

WRITE DOWN YOUR WORST FEARS

We humans are very vulnerable. Our lives can be upside down in an instant. On this page, you will imagine that your worst fears will come to life. For example, you have lost all your money and possessions. Worse, you have lost your health or beloved ones. It is now your job to listen and attend to all these fears. Write yourself a letter that captures your fears (below). Writing this letter may somehow have a bizarre liberating and cathartic effect on you.

THE BEST OF YOUR LEARNING has to come from YOUR OWN INITIATIVE

IT HAS TO BE SELF-DIRECTED LEARNING

KEEP YOUR BRAIN ACTIVE NOURISH IT EVERY DAY

RE-STRUCTURE YOUR JOB - RE-DESIGN IT 20% ME TIME YOUR INTERESTS YOUR PASSIONS

GET ENTREPRENEURIAL SEIZE OPPORTUNITIES DO SMART WORK

MINIMISE OR OUTSOURCE LOW LEVEL LOW VALUE LOW INTEREST ACTIVITIES

YOU HAVE TO BE CUTTING-EDGE IN WHAT YOU DO AND COMPETE WITH THE WORLD

COMBINE TWO-THREE SKILLS-COMPETENCE DOMAINS-KNOWLEDGE FIELDS TOGETHER

BE BETTER THAN 75% OF OTHER PEOPLE IN YOUR CORE COMPETENCES

WHAT ARE YOUR CORE COMPETENCES? RARE SKILLS THAT YOU ARE BETTER THAN MOST?

BORROW FROM A WIDE VARIETY OF FIELDS / AREAS

YOUR UNIQUE GIFTS/ TALENTS THAT YOU CAN LEVERAGE THAT HAS A VALUE IN THE MARKET PLACE?

OPENING DOORS, BUILDING BRIDGES

Pick an interesting county that you are not familiar with, but where you want to go, visit, or live in the future. Prepare a country kit or a presentation about that country.

Explore the best symbols, food, music, films, popular culture elements, universities, and cosmopolitan cities in your chosen country.

Find multimedia, web resources, and films about the country, its people, culture, and cities.

What is interesting about this culture and civilization? What are the top 10 things to explore, appreciate, and do in this country? Who are some of the "exceptional" people in this country who are globally known for their contributions to the world?

What is the "X factor" about this country? (What is the cool, interesting, "something" that makes for star quality or creates buzz?) Feel free to explore and find creative visuals, cultural insights, or fun facts.

YOUR GLOBAL VISION MAP

Design and create a vision map that enriches and expands the horizons of professionals operating in the global context of the 21st century. Your product can be a visual sketch page, a concept map, a framework, or a picture.

Think about the social, technological, economic, cultural, global trends emerging across different countries and cultures.

What does your big picture look like?

What are the new paradigms affecting the globe?

What are the major trends affecting world communities and societies?

These can be new terms or concepts related to management, organizations, business, leadership, society, science, technology, arts, politics, or global issues.

Try to come up with a holistic, futuristic and trans-disciplinary map of innovative and visionary trends or ideas.

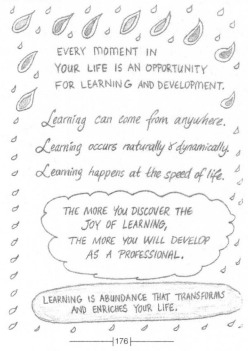

EVERY MOMENT IN YOUR LIFE IS AN OPPORTUNITY FOR LEARNING AND DEVELOPMENT.

Learning can come from anywhere.

Learning occurs naturally & dynamically.

Learning happens at the speed of life.

THE MORE YOU DISCOVER THE JOY OF LEARNING, THE MORE YOU WILL DEVELOP AS A PROFESSIONAL.

LEARNING IS ABUNDANCE THAT TRANSFORMS AND ENRICHES YOUR LIFE.

EXECUTIVE BOOK CLUB:

Read one book that captures your interest every week. Prepare your own executive summary for each book. Try to "zip" the content and message of the book into 1 page. This can also be a doodle or a concept map (see samples in the next few pages).

What is the core/essential message? What are the main points of discussion? Are there any cases or examples that strike you? How is this book different from others?

Why do you think is this book significant or useful? What is the promise? Implications or recommendations? How can you use this book?

What are the most interesting things/concepts/breakthrough ideas you have learned from this book?

MODERN AGE OF LASER BEAMS, TELECOMS, SATELLITES
MIND-BENDING IDEAS: SPACE-TIME CURVING, BIG BANG,
BLACK HOLES,   NEUTRON STARS
                                                      ATOMS

HOW CAN WE LEARN FROM THE GENIUS OF
EINSTEIN?

SCIENCES 1ST SUPERSTAR

$E=mc^2$

PHOTOELECTRIC EFFECT

GENERAL RELATIVITY

CAPTURING PUBLIC IMAGINATION

BIG SCIENCE

PEACE

ECLIPSES

THOUGHT EXPERIMENTS

① REMAIN IN TOUCH WITH YOUR CHILDLIKE
   CAPACITY FOR WONDER

② THINK IN PICTURES — IMAGINATION
   IS MORE IMPORTANT THAN KNOWLEDGE

③ YOU WILL ENCOUNTER ENORMOUS CHALLENGES—
   STICK TO RESILIENCE, HARD WORK, PERSISTENCE,
   TENACITY, CONFIDENCE, INDEPENDENCE

④ JUMP INTO UNKNOWN & UNCHARTED
   TERRITORY — DISCOVERY IS OUTSIDE BOUNDARIES

⑤ THINK GRAY IN FACE OF COMPLEXITY
   THINK FREE — BEYOND CONSTRAINTS

⑥ USE INTUITION, ARTS, HUMANITIES
   TO TAKE LEAPS OF IMAGINATION

⑦ BEST THEORIES ARE SIMPLE, PROFOUND &
                        BEAUTIFUL

Isaacson, W. (2008). *Einstein: His life and universe*. Simon and Schuster.

THE ONE THING by GARY KELLER AND JAY PAPASAN

You have to be
EXCELLENT (THE BEST)
in one thing that matters most
to you.

WHAT IS THAT ONE THING ?

THAT YOU WILL
① FOCUS
① DEVELOP EXPERTISE
① EXCEL/MASTER
① KEEP LEARNING
① BREAK YOUR RECORDS
① DO BEST
① CONTINUOUSLY IMPROVE
① SHARPEN YOUR SAW
① ENJOY
① GO DEEPER
① SPEND 10,000 HOURS
① BE THE BEST IN THE WORLD

THE 1 THING

Keller, G., & Papasan, J. (2013). *The one thing: The surprisingly simple truth behind extraordinary results.* Bard Press.

THE BUSINESS IDEA FACTORY   BY ANDRII SEDNIEV

- activate your BRAIN
- READ and get INSPIRED
- Your BRAIN should never be IDLE
- ask yourself QUESTIONS ?
- give your brain PROBLEMS to think about
- activate your SUPER-FAST brain
- ASK: WHY ?
- how can you make your life more PRODUCTIVE, CREATIVE, FULFILLING ?
- break a problem into small pieces and focus on each piece
- think in pictures diagrams
- THINK & REST after you generate lots of ideas & work hard; stop thinking about the problem
- SWITCH between Problems/tasks to refresh
- do not judge - produce tens of crazy ideas
- imagine
- make connections
- SLEEP REST DO OTHER THINGS — LET YOUR subconscious do the WORK

Sedniev, A. (2013). *The Business Idea Factory: A World-Class System for Creating Successful Business Ideas.* CreateSpace Independent Publishing Platform.

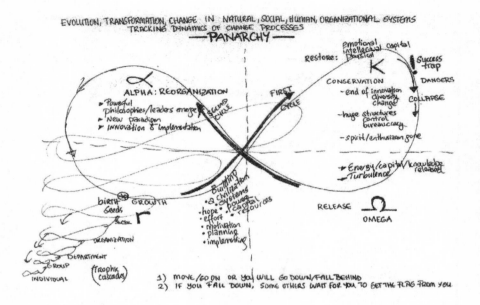

Gunderson, L. H. (2001). Panarchy: understanding transformations in human and natural systems. Island press.

Panarchy model is an interdisciplinary social science model used to capture human dynamics. I have adapted the model to explain the emotional dynamics in an individual's life (please see the individual panarchy model and its implications in the next page).

Here is your puzzle. Apply the panarchy model to your life. Reflect on your own experiences by tracking positive and negative phases/emotions in your life. Is this model helpful in explaining some of the dynamics? How do you cope with these different phases in your life?

α

- ● AS YOU RE-DESIGN & RE-BUILD YOUR LIFE, WHAT ARE YOUR PRIORITIES?
- ● WHICH ELEMENTS OF YOUR LIFE NEED TO CHANGE? WHY? HOW? WHERE DO YOU START?
- ● HOW WILL YOU PREVENT FUTURE FAILURES AND BUILD MORE RESILIENCE AND FLEXIBILITY AND DYNAMISM IN YOUR LIFE?
- ● WHAT WILL BE YOUR NEW PROJECT/VENTURE?
- ● BE COURAGEOUS IN TRANSFORMING YOUR LIFE - REDESIGN AND MAKE CHANGES AS NEEDED.
- → HOW AND WHERE DO YOU START LIVING YOUR 'NEW' LIFE?

K

- ● ENJOY YOUR SUCCESS, BUT ALSO DISRUPT YOURSELF AND YOUR STATUS QUO.
- ● INSTILL POCKETS OF LEARNING, CHANGE, AND INNOVATION IN YOUR LIFE.
- ● YOU MIGHT BE IN FAVOURABLE CONDITIONS NOW, BUT REMEMBER THAT IT MAY NOT LAST.
- ● PREPARE YOURSELF TO HARD TIMES. INVEST AND SAVE. REMEMBER: WINTER IS COMING!
- ● DO NOT LOOK DOWN ON PEOPLE. NEVER LOSE YOUR GRACE & HUMILITY.
- → HOW CAN YOU DISRUPT/CHANGE/RE-CREATE YOURSELF?

- ● WORK HARD, BUT DO NOT NEGLECT WORK-LIFE BALANCE.
- ● INSTILL POCKETS OF GRATIFICATION, JOY, AND HOBBIES IN YOUR LIFE.
- ● ATTEND TO QUALITY AND CREATIVE WORK.
- ● YOU ARE NOT A MACHINE. IT IS OK TO STOP, REFLECT, TAKE STOCK, SMELL THE ROSES.
- ● DEVELOP SMART GOALS AND WORK SMARTLY.
- → ARE YOU WORKING ON THE RIGHT GOALS?
- → WHERE DO YOU REALLY WANT TO BE?

r

- ● EVERYONE FAILS AT SOME POINT. IT IS YOUR TURN NOW. STOP PITYING YOURSELF - GET OVER IT!
- ● IT IS NOT THE END OF THE WORLD - BETTER DAYS WILL COME. DON'T LOSE HOPE.
- ● WHERE DID YOU DO WRONG? HOW CAN YOU LEARN FROM THIS EXPERIENCE?
- ● ROCK BOTTOM CAN BECOME A SOLID FOUNDATION (J. K. ROWLING)
- ● WRITE DOWN YOUR REFLECTIONS IN A DIARY.
- → WHO ARE YOU? WHAT IS THE MEANING OF ALL THIS? WHAT IS NEXT?

Ω

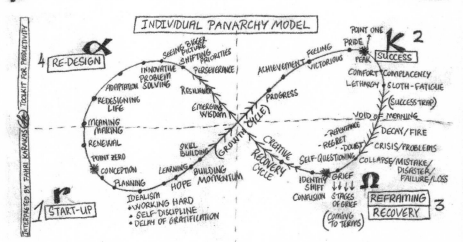

INDIVIDUAL PANARCHY MODEL

- ● HUMANS ARE DYNAMIC, OPEN, COMPLEX, ADAPTIVE, CHAOTIC, CREATIVE, SELF-DEFEATING, EMOTIONAL BEINGS.
- ● WE GO THROUGH POSITIVE AND NEGATIVE EMOTIONAL/PERSONAL CYCLES ALL THE TIME.
- ● WE HAVE TO KEEP MOVING: CHANGING, ADAPTING, INNOVATING, REDISCOVERING AND DISRUPTING OURSELVES.
- ● IF WE STOP LEARNING AND/OR MOVING, WE DO FAIL OR COLLAPSE BIG TIME.
- ● WHENEVER WE STOP MOVING, WE GO BACKWARDS AND THERE ARE OTHERS READY/WAITING TO TAKE THE FLAG FROM US.

Journey 6
THE GRIT & THE DRILL
Self-Regulation

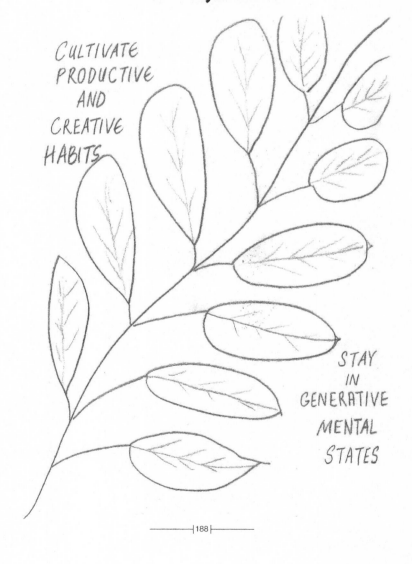

CULTIVATE
PRODUCTIVE
AND
CREATIVE
HABITS

STAY
IN
GENERATIVE
MENTAL
STATES

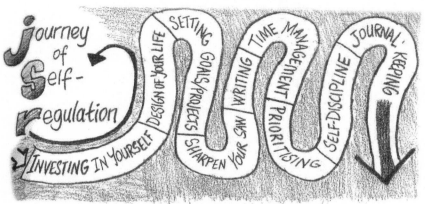

IMPROVING YOUR PRODUCTIVITY
THE GRIT AND THE DRILL

JOURNEY 6

In this journey;
- you will engage in planning & goal setting
- you will implement productivity hacks
- you will reflect on your time management
- you will improve your work & study habits

≪PRODUCTIVITY IS NEVER AN ACCIDENT. IT IS ALWAYS THE RESULT OF A COMMITMENT TO EXCELLENCE, INTELLIGENT PLANNING, AND FOCUSED EFFORT. ≫ —PAUL J. MEYER

" INVESTING IN YOURSELF IS THE MOST IMPORTANT INVESTMENT YOU WILL EVER MAKE IN YOUR LIFE... THERE'S NO FINANCIAL INVESTMENT THAT WILL EVER MATCH IT, BECAUSE IF YOU DEVELOP MORE SKILL, MORE ABILITY, MORE INSIGHT, MORE CAPACITY, THAT'S WHAT'S GOING TO REALLY MAKE THAT HAPPEN. "

WARREN BUFFETT'S ADVICE TO TONY ROBBINS,

TOOLS OF TITANS, p. 211
TIM FERRISS

INVESTING IN YOURSELF AND IN YOUR CAREER:
ONE DAY AT A TIME

Imagine your career is like a baby and you are the parent. You need to nurture it every day. How will you do it?

Imagine you are a shopkeeper. You need to open your store early every morning. Your 'store' is your career. How will you ensure that you are 'open for business' every day?

design
your life

THE DESIGN OF YOUR LIFE

Describe the life that you love and aspire to. Where do you want to live? You may describe how you spend your typical day. What elements make this day a happy day? How can you increase these elements in your current life?

Imagine that you have only five years left to live. What are your priorities now? Design your ideal life again.

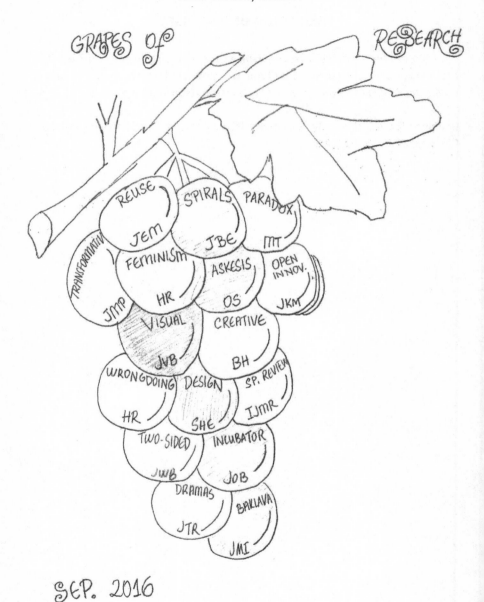

GRAPES OF RESEARCH

SEP. 2016

GRAPES OF JOYFUL PROJECTS

This was the 'Grape' of my own projects. Draw your own grape and list your career projects that you will work on during next year.

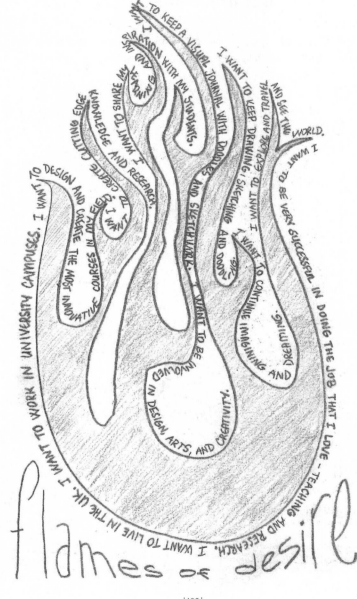

flames of desire

YOUR CAREER DESIRES AND
PROJECTS THET WILL FLAME THEM

Write about your career aspirations, desires, and dreams.

Come up with top 3 career projects you want to develop in the following months.

Think of possible titles for your career projects.

Do brainstorming and jot down your ideas in ways that inspire you.

In this imagination exercise, I have dreamed of the books that I could write one day.

AN EXERCISE IN IMAGINATION: WHAT WOULD YOU WRITE?

THE ART, SCIENCE & ENTREPRENEURSHIP OF
SELF-MAKING

DR. FAHRI KARAKAS

BENEVOLENT LEADERSHIP:
A GUIDE FOR WORLD-MAKING

DR. FAHRI KARAKAS

THE SKY IS THE LIMIT!
"IN PRAISE OF DREAMS AND IMAGINATION"

DR. FAHRI KARAKAS

QUO VADIS?
A CREATIVE AND VISUAL TOOLKIT FOR EMPLOYABILITY

DR. FAHRI KARAKAS

IMAGINE FOUR BOOK TITLES AND COVERS YOU'D WRITE

DREAM AND DESIGN THE COVERS AS YOU WISH

Come up with your own creative outputs or projects.
Design the posters or covers of those projects.

HERE ARE MY TITLES & BOOK COVERS:

THIS IS A POSITIVE AND BOUNDLESS SPACE

THIS IS THE OPPORTUNITY FOR DREAMING

MANIFESTO AGAINST PROCRASTINATION & LAZINESS

WHO PUSHES YOU INTO MEDIOCRITY & LAZINESS?

WHO IS Your Number 1 ENEMY?

WHO STOPS YOU?
WHO CRITICISES YOU?
WHO PREVENTS YOU

YOU!

It is an endless struggle.
If you want amazing things to happen;
you need self-discipline to sharpen your saw.
You need single-minded focus.
Sometimes, you will hate it and be tired.
Still, you need to show up and do your work
Sometimes, you will want to do
ANYTHING & EVERYTHING
to avoid that HARD TASK.
You need to EAT THAT FROG.
Do not wait for inspiration for
writing and producing. Do the f******
WORK!

CHALLENGE YOURSELF. STRETCH. GROW.

SHARPEN YOUR SAW

Even if you love your job, there will be times that you hate what you are doing. There are punitive moments in every job - even dream jobs.

Golden Hours: 6.00 to 11.00 a.m.
Get your coffee and start early
If you cannot focus at home, go to the library
Allow 2-3 hour sessions for serious writing work
Allow yourself some time to get into the writing task
Even if you have 15 minutes, you can do some small work for your article or thesis (organize references, find 1-2 more resources, write an abstract etc.)
Avoid bad habits (excessive Internet, TV, Facebook..)
Have breaks and refresh yourself: Hobbies, sports, friends, fruit, chocolate, prayer...

I have used strategies above to make progress in my academic writing. What could be your specific strategies to make progress on your most significant projects?

STAGES OF A WRITING PROJECT
by FAHRI KARAKAS

PROCRASTINATION	Oh I still have a LOT of time...	I can worry about this later.	It would be really GOOD if I started..
PANICKING	OMG Time is ticking..	THE DEADLINE is APPROACHING FAST!	I really need to START!
PLANNING	Oh this is really TOUGH!	How will I manage & sort this out?	I need to WORK SMART & EFFECTIVELY!
STARTING WRITING	Oh this is SO SLOW!	BUT at least I have a plan & I started writing.	I need to work incredibly hard!
PROGRESSING WRITING	Oh I am stuck - nothing works	I need new ways of thinking, writing, problem solving.	I need to keep working and continue the momentum
MOMENTUM REVISING	Oh I think I can finish this!	More coffee. Less sleep. FOCUS. intense camp. Write.Write.Write	Revise, revise, revise. Now I am getting somewhere :)

WRITING IS LIKE CLIMBING A MOUNTAIN

- NEVER GIVE UP.
- KEEP MOVING.
- HUGE PROJECTS START WITH SMALL STEPS
- IT IS NEVER EASY.
- FIGHT YOURSELF TO DO BETTER

KEEP WRITING.

TIME MANAGEMENT GRID EXERCISE

You can categorise your activities and tasks based on two questions:
1) Is this task urgent?
2) Is this task important?

Based on the combination of answers, you can end up in 4 quadrants:

Quadrant 1: Urgent & important (emergencies, deadlines..)

Quadrant 2: Not urgent but important (skill and knowledge development, quality of life issues, long term projects, learning..)

Quadrant 3: Urgent but not important (grocery shopping, meetings, paying bills or rent..)

Quadrant 4: Not important, nor urgent (wasting time, binge-watching on Netflix, Facebook..)

In this exercise, you will think about the activities and tasks you have been involved during past week. Come up with at least 5 activities for each quadrant. For each activity, write down how many hours you spent for that activity (in parentheses).

After finishing your list, analyse your patterns in time management. What did you learn from this exercise? How can you improve your time management?

Urgent and important

Not urgent but important

Urgent but not important

Not important, nor urgent

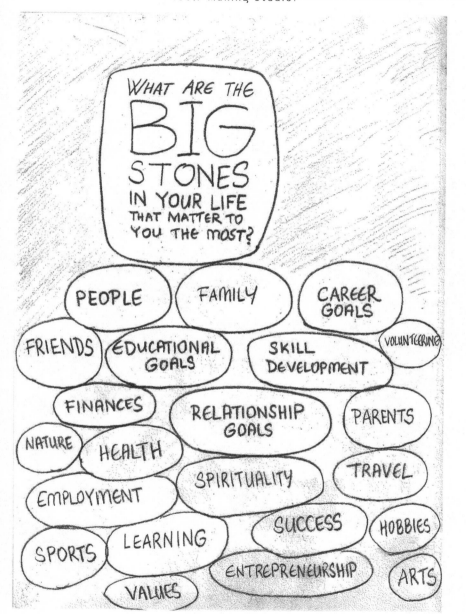

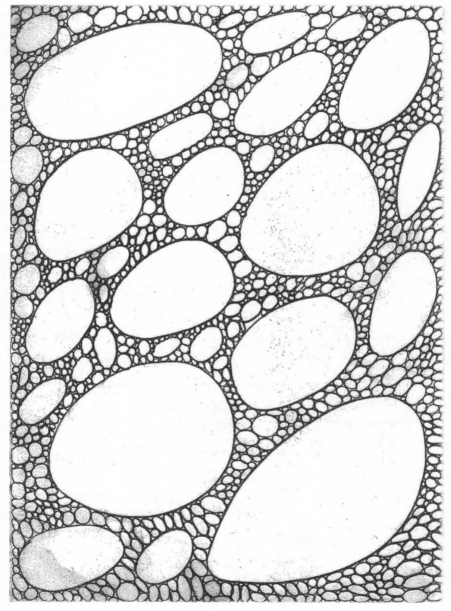

MORNING REFLECTION

Please write your responses below:

1) Make a list of minimum 10 things that you should be grateful for.

1
2
3
4
5
6
7
8
9
10

2) When did you last feel curious, playful, and excited? How can you increase these 'magical moments' in your daily life?

3) If money was not a factor, how would you spend your life?

4) If your life were 120 years long and you would choose four different careers, what would you like to do? Imagine four scenarios (think of lives or jobs that would be fun and exciting to have).

5) If you were able to take one year out to learn a new skill, what would you learn?

6) If you do not worry about failure or self-image, what might you try doing?

7) If you could only work 1 hour for your business or project on one day; what would you do during that hour?

1. GET UP EARLY. 5.00 AM TO 10.00 AM ARE THE GOLDEN HOURS

2. HAVE A NICE BREAKFAST. DRINK STRONG COFFEE.

3. DIVE IN. EAT THE FROG.

4. USE TIMERS TO FOCUS ON YOUR HARD TASKS

5. KEEP MORNING PAGES

6. AVOID SOCIAL MEDIA AND MINDLESS SURFING

7. PRIORITIZE AND IMPLEMENT PRIORITY TASKS.

8. USE CHECKLISTS. FINISH TASKS.

9. INSPIRE YOURSELF. KEEP LEARNING.

10. KEEP THE FLOW AND MOMENTUM

PRODUCTIVE HABITS for BRIGHT MORNINGS

DESIGNING YOUR WEEK

You will use the next page to design your upcoming work week. You will classify all your tasks and activities (that you will do over the course of this week) into one of these four quadrants

•FROGS: These are your deadlines—urgent and important tasks (such as emergencies or application deadlines).

•LIONS: These are long term skill building, knowledge, development activities and tasks (i.e. investing in yourself, your career, and your quality of life). You need to make sure to prioritise these tasks (even though there is no deadline) and make sure to schedule ample time for these tasks.

•BUGS: These are small (or big) daily tasks (things to do) that you have to do anyway. They might include shopping, cleaning the house, cooking, laundry, invoices/bills, bureaucracy, attending meetings, phone calls, family chores etc. Use a checklist to keep track of your progress on these tasks and get them done. Do these tasks when you are mentally tired.

•BUTTERFLIES: These are rewarding activities that are exciting or refreshing for you (i.e. you look forward to them). These might include hobbies, arts, fun activities, creative or inspirational projects, Netflix or cinema, meeting friends, picnic, spa, walks in nature, travel, or parties. Make sure you schedule these mini-holidays or escapes and spend several hours on these leisure or relaxation activities.

FROGS

URGENT + IMPORTANT PROJECTS

LIONS

LONG TERM STRATEGIC PROJECTS

BUGS

DAILY TASKS & OPERATIONS

BUTTERFLIES

PARALLEL CAREERS-HOBBIES-FUN

LEARNING AT THE SPEED OF LIFE

What's the most interesting thing you have read or seen this week?

What are your hard-won skills? What is the hardest thing you have achieved? How did you achieve it?

Do you learn something every day that you enjoy, can use, or just love? If not, how can you create structure for yourself and ensure that you keep learning every day?

What are inspiring innovative ideas you have recently encountered?

Which seminars or workshops can you attend and which books can you read to expand your knowledge and skills in your career and/or personal life? Make a list and a budget.

How can you be a good storyteller? What could be three good stories about your life that you can share that entertain or engage people?

How can you approach all places, people, and ideas with a sense of discovery and learning? Where is the mystery or the magic? How can you sustain that sense of enchantment in your life?

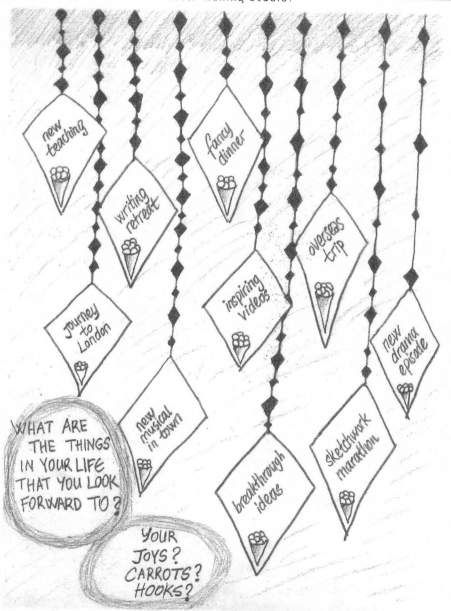

Journey 7
THE TEDDY BEAR & THE BOOST
Self-Compassion

*your vulnerability
is precious —
it is the source of courage,
authenticity and creativity*

AND JOY, LOVE, OPENNESS, AND CARE

AND HOPE, PRAYER, AND SPIRITUALITY

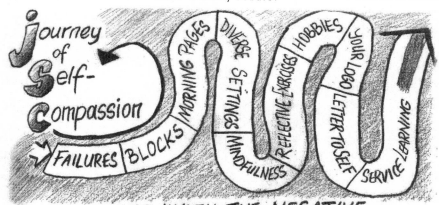

DEALING WITH THE NEGATIVE
THE TEDDY BEAR AND THE BOOST

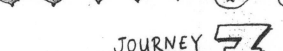

JOURNEY 7

In this journey;
- you will reflect on what holds you back
- you will learn methods to cope with stress
- you will reflect on your failures & turn them into learning & development
- you will work on your mental well-being

《SUCCESS IS STUMBLING FROM FAILURE TO FAILURE WITH NO LOSS OF ENTHUSIASM.》

《SUCCESS IS NOT FINAL, FAILURE IS NOT FATAL: IT IS THE COURAGE TO CONTINUE THAT COUNTS.》

—WINSTON CHURCHILL

sometimes life will be messy
and complicated.
be curious and learn to solve
experimental   problems.
there will be twists and turns.
it will look impossible until you
resolve it.
enjoy the puzzle and the journey

CELEBRATING FAILURES

Recount your biggest failures. Did you learn from these failures? What did you learn? Can you celebrate these failures - since they have probably helped you grow? Write down your reflections below to make peace with your failures.

I have written this page when I was really annoyed with myself as a result of my lack of progress on a difficult writing project.

URGHH!

OFFF!

🤯 I have an ~~important~~ impending deadline.

However, I have managed to escape from serious work for days – even weeks.

I feel ready to escape from this task and

I procrastinate in a stubborn, painstaking manner.

It is as if I am ready & willing to do anything but this work.

I find myself lost in hours of binge-watching TV dramas and useless Internet surfing.

I feel a terrible guilt, but my desire to indulge in "idleness" & "stupidity" continues.

I have to break this vicious cycle.

SMALL STEPS.

SMALL ACHIEVEMENTS.

LONG WAY TO GO.

START WALKING. WORKING.

GET UP. MOVE. STUDY.

WHAT BLOCKS YOU? WHY ARE YOU NOT PROGRESSING? WRITE DOWN THE ISSUES. THINK OF SOLUTIONS.

How do you limit yourself? How can you stop it?

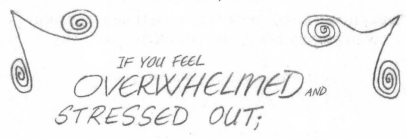

IF YOU FEEL
OVERWHELMED AND
STRESSED OUT;

1. WRITE MORNING PAGES - WRITE WHATEVER COMES INTO YOUR MIND. WRITE FOR 20 MINUTES. THIS IS YOUR STREAM OF CONSCIOUSNESS. IT CAN BE PURELY CHAOTIC AND RANDOM. THESE PAGES ARE ONLY FOR YOUR EYES - KEEP THEM SECRET. WRITING THEM WILL SET YOUR MIND FREE. WRITE DOWN YOUR STRESSORS, FEARS, ANXIETIES, AND NEGATIVE EMOTIONS. ALSO WRITE ABOUT WHAT YOU NEED TO DO.

2. GIVE A BREAK. GIVE YOURSELF A TREAT. TAKE A WALK. TAKE DEEP BREATHS. FORGIVE YOURSELF. ·PLAN A MINI-VACATION FOR YOURSELF. GET SUPPORT FROM YOUR FRIENDS. FIND TIME TO THINK. REFRESHING YOURSELF WILL ALLOW YOU TO BE MORE PRODUCTIVE.

3. DO A LIST OF THINGS THAT YOU HAVE DONE AND THAT YOU WILL DO. DELVE INTO HARD WORK - START WORKING. TAKE SMALL STEPS. GET MOMENTUM.

KEEP CALM
AND
MOVE ON

Julia Cameron's classic book is full of a lot of practical wisdom and useful exercises for creatives such as writing morning pages. Read more: Cameron, J. (2016). *The artist's way.* Penguin.

WRITE YOUR FIRST MORNING PAGE HERE

IMMERSE YOURSELF IN DIVERSE SETTINGS

When you feel stressed out or tired, try changing your rhythm and context. Immerse yourself in diverse and unusual settings (i.e. visit a design museum, participate in a jazz concert, attend a wedding ceremony, volunteer at a hospital, or have a picnic).

Hobbies as diverse as poetry, skydiving, storytelling, yoga, and dancing may be refreshing for you. You can find new insights, fresh ideas, and inspiration when you travel across different contexts or cultures. To achieve out-of-the-box thinking, you need to travel outside your box (or mental walls).

How will you escape the rut? Where will you go this week? What will be your new activities?

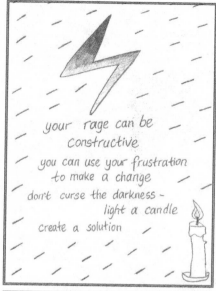

your rage can be
constructive

you can use your frustration
to make a change

don't curse the darkness -
light a candle

create a solution

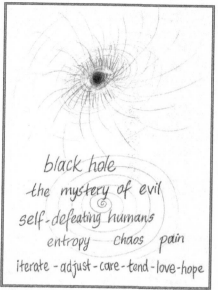

black hole

the mystery of evil

self-defeating humans

entropy — chaos pain

iterate - adjust - care - tend - love - hope

Sometimes, you will fail
you are not a failure

embrace failure
use it for learning
do not stop trying
move on
begin again
fail early & often - learn from
your mistakes.

HATRED CORRUPTION INEQUALITY
OPPRESSION POVERTY INJUSTICE
TYRANNY
TEARS
WARS BOMBS TERROR
REFUGEES HUNGRY CHILDREN
SUFFERING ATROCITIES SYRIA
IRAQ

there is pain & injustice
everywhere
Sufferers, victims, children,
families...
what can you do about them?
how can you help?

HOW CAN YOU KEEP YOUR SANITY & LIVE
EVERYDAY LIFE ?

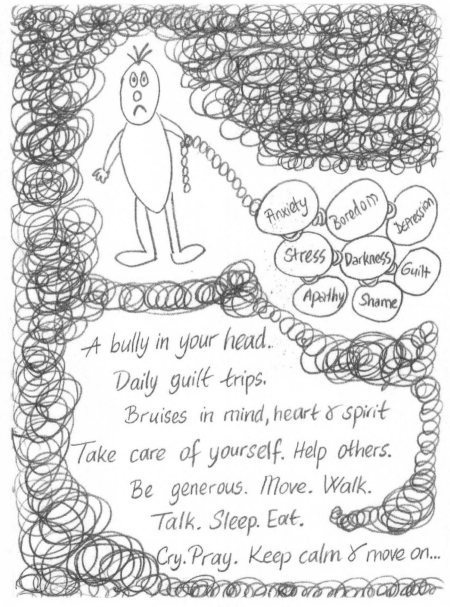

Anxiety
Boredom
Depression
Stress
Darkness
Guilt
Apathy
Shame

A bully in your head..
Daily guilt trips.
Bruises in mind, heart & spirit
Take care of yourself. Help others.
Be generous. Move. Walk.
Talk. Sleep. Eat.
Cry. Pray. Keep calm & move on...

COPING WITH STRESS: MINDFULNESS EXERCISE

You often work and live in a frenzied rush that demands swift decision-making and action. With increasing demands and time pressures, it becomes more and more difficult for you to maintain focus, to slow down and reflect, to search for the deeper meaning, and feel what your heart wants.

One remedy for this problem is allowing enough time and space for reflection and mindfulness. Slow down. Spend 10 minutes for your "being mode" - engage in silent contemplation, meditation, and deep breaths.

ONLY I CAN MAKE A POSITIVE CHANGE IN MY LIFE. I HAVE TO START SOMEWHERE. SMALL STEPS. EVEN IF I HATE IT, I HAVE TO TRY. I KNOW IT IS PAINFUL BUT I HAVE TO HANG IN THERE. AT LEAST I AM TRYING AND I AM ON MY WAY.

THIS IS MY JOURNEY AND I CAN SHAPE AND DESIGN THIS JOURNEY. ON THE WAY, I WILL FALL DOWN AND GET UP AGAIN. I WILL LEARN AND GROW AS A PERSON. IN EACH STEP, I WILL BE A BETTER PERSON.

I WILL WORK REALLY HARD AND GIVE ALL MY EFFORTS AND TIME AND ENERGY. I WILL COMPETE WITH MYSELF AND CHALLENGE MYSELF EVERY DAY.

I AM READY TO GET TIRED AND FEEL INTIMIDATED AND CHALLENGED. EACH DIFFICULTY FORCES ME TO GROW AS A PROBLEM SOLVER. I WILL NOT QUIT.

I DO MY JOB BETTER AND BETTER EVERY DAY. I AM RESOURCEFUL, RESILIENT, AND CREATIVE. I AM MAKING A DIFFERENCE.

IT IS NOT THE DESTINATION, BUT IT IS THE PROCESS. BLOODY HARD WORK.

BE GROW IMPROVE PROGRESS SMELL THE ROSES KEEP LEARNING ADAPTING, INNOVATING

FAHRI KARAKAS 2017©

Self-Making Studio

REFLECTIVE EXERCISE ON YOUR FAILURES

As J. K. Rowling beautifully explains, 'hitting the rock bottom' can become 'a solid foundation to rebuild your life'.

Failure can be inevitable, but it is valuable. It can be a powerful tool for your learning, growth and development.

What were your biggest disappointments and/or failures in the last 3 years?

What did you learn from these mistakes?

Can you construct positive personal narratives that emerge from these mistakes?

Sometimes things happen.
Negative things.
You lose your morale and motivation.
You do not even feel like moving your finger.
You just want to escape from all.
Hide under the blanket and sleep all day.
Binge watching and procrastination.
Give yourself time.
Forgive yourself. Things will get
BETTER.

TOOLS OF TITANS
p. 570
TIM FERRISS

JAR OF AWESOME

IF ANYTHING COOL, EXCITING, JOYFUL, GREAT HAPPENS TODAY,
WRITE IT ON A PIECE OF PAPER, PUT A DATE, PUT IT
IN THE JAR. (ALL SUCCESSES, SMALL WINS, JOYS, HAPPY MOMENTS)
PUT SOMETHING IN THE JAR EVERY DAY.

*this will help you feel grateful over time
and remember happy moments*

REFLECTIVE EXERCISE ON BLOCKS AND UNBLOCKING

What are the top 3 challenges or blocks that prevent your progress in your ideal career?

Create and design 3 solutions for each.

What would inspire/motivate you?

What do you need to do differently?

If you are stuck, consider asking yourself questions and trying to answer them (this will create a conversation and a momentum).

If you cannot find a solution, go for a long walk. Long walks are a good way to solve or process problems.

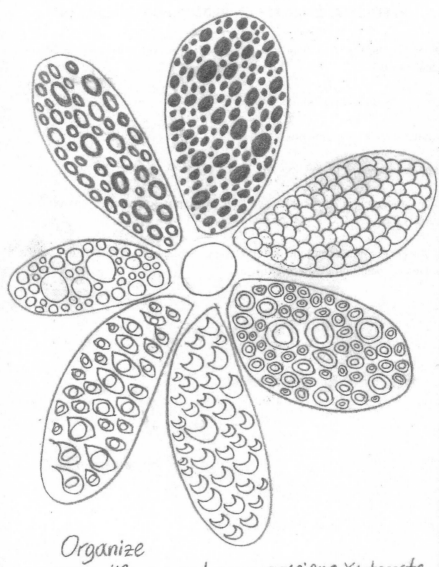

Organize
your life around your passions & interests

YOUR HOBBIES AS PARALLEL CAREERS

Hobbies can be a parallel career for you. Follow your interests and hobbies professionally or artistically.

Do not make perfect plans - implement and take action and make mistakes.

What are your hobbies?

Organise a weekly 'date with yourself'. Organise a weekly 'date with yourself'. Julia Cameron, author of 'The Artist's Way' calls these as 'artist dates' and recommends you to do these 2-3 hours every week and alone.

DESIGN YOUR OWN LOGO

Take 2-3 minutes to come up with possible different concepts for your own logo.

Think of symbols and metaphors that convey the essence of you as a person.

Why is this concept/symbol meaningful to you? How and why does it represent you?

Choose a design you like best. Sketch it by hand or design it digitally.

How is this logo linked to your values and personal brand?

You can include a motto or slogan if you want.

WRITE A LETTER TO YOURSELF

Write an inspirational letter to yourself below. Write about your values and principles. Write about your dreams. Date the letter.

DEAR FAHRI,
GET OUT OF THE RUT.
CLEAR OUT WEEDS.
GROW AND CULTIVATE YOUR WRITING.
YOUR ATTENTION IS PRECIOUS.
DO NOT WASTE IT.
KEEP CALM AND KEEP WRITING.
KEEP LEARNING AND KEEP TEACHING.
YOU HAVE NOT CREATED YOUR
MASTERPIECES YET.
INVEST YOUR WHOLE TIME, ENERGY, ATTENTION
AND HARD WORK. LIKE A FARMER.
SOW THE SEEDS.
WATER THEM.
GROW THEM WITH LOVE AND EFFORT.
SUCH IS THE JOY OF A LIFE OF HARD WORK.
HONEST HARD WORK.
SMART WORK.
KEEP WORKING.

clock is ticking!

▷ you are entering a very
busy era that
will strengthen you if
you work smartly and
really hard.
YOU HAVE TO SET UP INCREDIBLY
DISCIPLINED WRITING SESSIONS.
▷ use your brain all the time
▷ develop your skill set &
cutting edge knowledge
▷ continue writing and
publishing.
▷ remember your theory
paper/comps writing days.

DESIGN YOUR SERVICE-LEARNING PROJECT

You are tasked with making the world a better place. Where would you start? Reflect on yourself, your values, your social responsibility, and your role in the global world. Reflect on the world's most important problems, your career, and your strengths. Try to find a project area that is at the intersection of these (You can learn more on these topics if you Google '80.000 Hours').

Brainstorm and find an innovative project which could change the world around you. This can be an NGO proposal or a social innovation project that will have a positive impact on the lives of people.

Choose a country. What will you be your contribution in this country? What will be your role in achieving and sustaining positive change? What can you do in your sphere of influence to make a positive impact?

build bridges of understanding
be a rainbow in someone else's cloud

MAYA ANGELOU

Journey 8
THE SIGHTS & THE SOUNDS
Self and the City

a creative

diary

by
DR FAHRI KARAKAS

You are more creative
when you are FREE !

free from : ROUTINES
STRESS
SELF HATE
BLAME
GUILT
POINTLESS INTERNET
BINGE WATCHING
E-MAILS
POLITICS
COMPLAINING
LAZINESS
PROCRASTINATION

TODAY WAS 28TH OF APRIL, 2016.
I CAME TO LONDON YESTERDAY EVENING
FOR MY TEACHING AT MOUNTBATTEN &
STAYED IN A FRIEND'S PLACE LAST NIGHT.
IT HAS BEEN ONE OF 'THOSE DAYS' -
FULL OF INSPIRATION, HOPE, AND LOVELY MEMORIES.
WE WORKED AT LSE AND SAW THE PLAY 'RAILWAY CHILDREN'
AT KING'S THEATRE FEATURING A TRAIN STATION STAGE &
A REAL STEAM ENGINE TRAIN. WE WANDERED AROUND
COVENT GARDEN, BOUGHT LOVELY STATIONERY, AND ATE
A SCRUMPULOUS CAKE AT BALTHAZAR'S.

SO MANY LIGHTBULBS
EUREKA MOMENTS
SOURCES OF INSPIRATION !

I LOVE SERTAG ♡ I LOVE LONDON

DO
WHAT
YOU
LOVE

LOVE
WHAT
YOU
DO

FIND YOUR PASSION !
FOLLOW YOUR HEART !

each white page
is an opportunity.

you can design, draw, write
WHATEVER
you want !

each day is like a white page in your life.

THE CHOICES ARE YOURS.
IT IS YOUR LIFE.
TAKE INITIATIVE.

BALIKESİR 1985 - 1996

BALIKESİR
is the city
I discovered the larger WORLD
first

SIRRI YIRCALI
ANADOLU LİSESİ
BALIKESİR
1984

SAT KULESİ   İMAM BİRLİ   LEARNING ENGLISH   DISCOVERIES

KES   KAZDAĞI   SYAL   ÜNİV. HAZIRLIK ÖSS-ÖYS   ZAĞNOS

LUK   KOLONYA   ZEYTİN   BENGİ   GUARBI

DA   EDREMİT   HÖŞMERİM   DEĞİRMEN BOĞAZI   ALTI EYLÜL YURDU   CUM. LİSESİ   GÜNDOĞAN

HASANBOĞULDU

REFLECTION
WHEN DID YOU FIRST ESTABLISH YOUR LIFE AWAY FROM YOUR FAMILY? HOW DID YOU MANAGE THIS?

WHICH PERIOD IN YOUR LIFE WAS CHARACTERIZED BY TRANSFORMATION? YOUR TRANSITION 'FROM CATERPILLAR TO BUTTERFLY'?

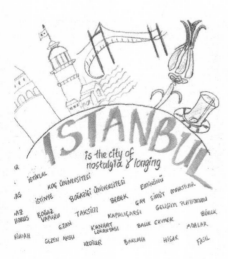

ISTANBUL
is the city of
nostalgia & longing

IR   İSTİKLAL   KOÇ ÜNİVERSİTESİ

AŞ   İSTİNYE   BOĞAZİÇİ ÜNİVERSİTESİ   BEBEK   EMİNÖNÜ

AZ   BOĞAZ VAPURU   TAKSİM   KAPALIÇARŞI   GAY SİMİT MANZARA.   GELİŞİM PLATFORMU

HORUS   EZAN   KANAAT LOKANTASI   BALIK EKMEK   BÖREK

KIMAH   GEZEN AKSU   KEDİLER   BAKLAVA   HİSAR   ADALAR   FASIL

REFLECTION
THINK ABOUT THE PLACES AND SPACES WHERE YOU FEEL ALIVE. WHERE DO YOU THRIVE? WHY?

LISTEN TO YOUR HEART. NOURISH YOUR SPIRIT. WHEN WAS THE LAST TIME YOU FELT AT PEACE WITH YOURSELF? WHAT WERE YOU DOING?

LONDON
inspires me!

SICALS
THEATRE UNIVERSITIES LEARNING. BANKSY
SLUMS COVENT GARDEN ENTREPRENEURSHIP BOROUGH MARKET
S TECHNOLOGY COFFEE SHAKESPEARE AFTERNOON TEA FRIENDS ST PAUL'S
HLOCK RESTAURANTS DESIGN CREATIVITY DIVERSITY

REFLECTION
WHICH CITIES & PLACES INSPIRE YOU? WHY?

THINK OF SOME ACTIVITIES & EXPERIENCES THAT YOU LOOK FORWARD TO IN THIS CITY/PLACE.

NORWICH
is where I lived & work

N CITY
CITY NORWICH MARKET NORWICH LANES GROSVENOR'S FISH BAR
EDRAL WENSUM RIVER UEA UNESCO CITY OF LITERATURE BIVOU
ROUDS ELM'S HILL NORWICH BUSINESS SCHOOL NORWICH RESEARCH PARK CASTLE
LK RIVERSIDE WALK NORWICH 12 LEISURE
S CARSTONE CHAPELFIELD THE FORUM ARTS CRAFTS CULTURE

REFLECTION
DO YOU EXPLORE THE CITY YOU ARE LIVING IN?
WHEN WAS THE LAST TIME YOU CHASED ADVENTURES LIKE A TOURIST?

WHAT ARE YOUR TOP ACTIVITIES? TOP SPOTS?
HOW DO YOU REVITALIZE & REFRESH YOURSELF?

REFLECTION

WHAT IS YOUR TOP DREAM THAT YOU WANT TO REALIZE? HOW CAN YOU MAKE IT COME TRUE?

IMAGINE YOU FOLLOWED YOUR DREAMS, TOOK RISKS, WENT FOR ADVENTURE, REACHED FOR THE STARS. WRITE THE HEADLINES FOR THE NEWS ARTICLE FEATURING YOUR SUCCESS STORY BELOW.

REFLECTION

IN WHICH SPACES & CONTEXTS CAN YOU UNLEASH YOUR OWN CREATIVITY?

FROM WHICH FIELDS CAN YOU BORROW IDEAS & INSPIRATION FOR YOUR JOB/TASKS? THINK OF DIVERSE FIELDS & IDEAS.

AMSTERDAM

is the city for relaxing escapes

GOGH MUSEUM

FRANK HOUSE   KEIZERSGRACHT

AAN   REMBRANDT   FLOWER MARKET

HEINEKEN   RIJKSMUSEUM   DUTCH CHEESE   THE AMSTEL

SINGEL   VAN GOGH

CYCLING

CANAL CRUISE

TULIPS

VONDELPARK

EYE FILM INSTITUTE

REFLECTION

WHAT ARE SOME OF YOUR FAVORITE SPOTS OR PLACES THAT YOU PREFER FOR HOLIDAY? HOW DO YOU UNWIND?

WHICH HOBBIES OR ACTIVITIES DO YOU PREFER TO ENERGIZE & REVITALIZE YOURSELF? MAKE A PLAN TO PUT THEM INTO ACTION.

ATHENS

is the city of arts, philosophy, and drama

HENON

CROPOLIS

A   AGORA   SYNTAGMA SQUARE   MOUNT LYCABETTUS

PLE OF PIAN ZEUS   OLYMPIC GAMES   OLIVE TREES   MONASTRAKI

PIRAEUS   FARMERS MARKET   OMONOIA   ACROPOLIS MUSEUM

TAVERNA

GABI   GYRO

SOUVLAKI

FAVA

IRINI

SPANAKOPITA

REFLECTION

WHAT PATTERNS CAN YOU LEARN FROM ANCIENT CIVILIZATIONS ON VIRTUOUS & SUSTAINABLE LIVING?

HOW CAN YOU ENRICH YOUR LIFE THROUGH GOOD FOOD, GOOD MUSIC & GOOD CULTURE & GOOD FRIENDS?

BEIRUT *is a city of surprises and chaotic delights*

ICHE
BARLIVA
KEBBE
AL-AMARI MOSQUE
ON ROCKS
JEITA GROTTO
SHAMARM
EIRUT SOUKS
THE CORNICHE
SAIFI VILLAGE
AMERICAN UNIVERSITY IN BEIRUT
FALAFEL
A
ZAITUNAY BAY
MUHAMMAD AL-AMIN MOSQUE
SANAYEH GARDEN
BAHSAS TREE
CATS
SAHLAB
ET
MMAEL GEMMAYZEH
ST NICHOLAS STAIRS
BYBLOS
JOUNIEH
HARISSA
SOUK AL TAYEB

REFLECTION

HOW CAN YOU NAVIGATE CHAOS & COMPLEXITY?
HOW CAN YOU THRIVE IN TURBULENCE?

WHAT CAN YOU LEARN FROM DIVERSE CULTURES & RELIGIONS?
WHAT ARE YOUR TIPS FOR LIVING TOGETHER IN HARMONY?

EXERCISE: A PERSONAL CITY JOURNAL
Cities and their meaning in your life

•Briefly respond to the reflective questions in the preceding pages (15 minutes)
•Looking at the example doodle pages, create your own list of cities that are meaningful in your life (10 minutes)
•You can include cities that you have lived or worked in
•You can also include cities that you have visited or you have been inspired by.
•You can also draw doodles like I did (if you like, just for fun)
•About each city, revisit and list all the key words, emotions, institutions, people, food, famous sights, places, or symbols that come to your mind.
•For each city, write about what you have learned and how you have grown in that city (20 minutes)

EPILOGUE

What did you learn from this toolkit?

What are the top things that you will implement (that emerge from these pages)?

Did you try out new practices or activities that are recommended in these pages? What were they? How did they turn out?

What are some of your most memorable reflections or surprising insights about yourself that emerged across these pages?

As a result of these reflections and new insights gained, how can you go forward?

How can you create your ideal work space? When are you most productive and creative? Are you a late night person or an early morning person? How can you get into the writing/creating mood? How can you create your own ways?

GOING FORWARD

Find and purchase your ideal notebook - this is your luxury. Keep it with you at all times. Capture your ideas, goals, and thoughts as they emerge. How can you best practice diary keeping and note-taking in your life? Identify some practical action points below.

How can you make a habit of doodling, drawing, or sketching out new ideas as they emerge? What could be some interesting ideas or projects to explore and play with?

How can you open up yourself and your mind to new people, ideas, interests, experiences, and adventures?

How can you allocate more time for daydreaming, playing, reading, imagining and learning? How can you create your own structure and rituals to ensure your involvement in these activities?

How will you sustain your sense of learning, enchantment, and curiosity in your life?

KICKSTART YOUR LIFE

How can you achieve a new wave of creative, distinctive, and impactful work in your life and in your career?   Write down your strategy and manifesto below.

POSTER FOR CHANGE

Prepare an inspirational poster for yourself now (use space below). You can put this poster on your work space or study wall.

by FAHRI KARAKAS 2018©

The world is changing very fast. We need to change and adapt rapidly. We need to DISRUPT ourselves.	Change is never easy. It is scary and uncomfortable. We need to stretch and CHALLENGE ourselves. We need to get out of our comfort zone.	There is no linear career path. Forget the career ladder. The job market is ever shifting. It is a jungle out there. Prepare for the GIG ECONOMY. Be FLEXIBLE.	It is your responsibility to design your life, your career and your world. Act as an entrepreneur, innovator, designer, and artist.	Your career is your start-up - your baby. Nurture and nourish it every day. Invest in your learning, skill development, training, experiences and KNOWLEDGE. Invest in yourself.	Ignore everyone and their expectations. This is YOUR LIFE. Be WEIRD. Do things that will EXCITE you. ENJOY your life. Dare to dream. Dare to disappoint others.
Learning is life's greatest gift and adventure. KEEP LEARNING fresh, exciting, amazing things every day. Share them with others.	Experiment and take chances and risks. Failures are OK. Learn from your failures. Develop RESILIENCE and bounce back (forward:)	Do not settle with easy, visible or conventional path(s) ahead of you. Avoid the crowds. Go FOR LESS TRAVELLED ROUTE. Discover uncharted territory (BLUE OCEANS)	Everyone is born creative (and given crayons). Rediscover, reclaim, unleash, and nourish YOUR CREATIVE INNER CHILD ('genie')	Leverage your STRENGTHS instead of fixing your weaknesses. Harness your unique TALENTS, SKILLS, BACKGROUND. Use your gifts to CREATE something AMAZING.	Creativity and IMAGINATION are boundless resources. Tap into them. Be hungry, naive, foolish. Open your mind to new perspectives. Create for the sheer love of it.
Develop your "INSPIRATIONAL CAPITAL" - your capabilities of enchantment, wonder & reflection. Follow your INTERESTS, HOBBIES & CURIOSITIES. Find your mojo.	Where is your heart? What do you LOVE doing? Find your own voice. Discover your PASSIONS. Create your masterpieces. Engage in "LABOUR OF LOVE"	Life's best moments are when you work hard and experience FLOW, to accomplish something difficult and worthwhile. Produce your BEST WORK (honest hard work).	Climb your own Everest. Do not compare yourself to others. Compete with yourself. Make sure you achieve progress (even 1%) every day. Don't wait for "approval". Be the best in what you do.	Develop your personal brand - build a good reputation & network. Create value and bring your best contribution. Tell interesting stories that show who you are and where you come from.	Life is beyond disciplines & borders. Be a Renaissance person. Imagine, play, learn, create, focus, improvise, design, and improve. Be resourceful and resilient. Show up. Be present.

This is the manifesto and summary of this book. I know this poster is very small (sorry:), but your challenge is to go over and pay attention to these principles. How can you implement these principles in your life? Come up with a small action for each principle.

RECOMMENDED MOVIES

This is my personal list of inspirational films on creativity and self-making.

- Art and Copy (Documentary)
- Inception
- Birdman or (The Unexpected Virtue of Ignorance)
- Pleasantville
- Erin Brockovich
- Groundhog Day
- The Pursuit of Happyness
- Shawshank Redemption
- A Beautiful Mind
- A Theory of Everything
- The Imitation Game
- Eat Pray Love
- Good Will Hunting
- Dead Poets Society
- Ratatouille
- It's a Wonderful Life
- The Help
- Big Fish
- Whiplash
- Patch Adams
- October Sky
- Life is Beautiful
- Hidden Figures
- Joy
- Julie and Julia
- Billy Elliot
- The Social Network
- The Corporation (Documentary)
- Wonder
- Bill Cunningham: New York (Documentary)
- The Up Series (1964-2012)
- Jiro Dreams of Sushi
- Chef's Table (Documentary)
- Capital C (Documentary)

FURTHER RESOURCES

Recommended Journals
- Harvard Business Review
- Sloan Management Review

Recommended Newspapers and Magazines
- Wired
- The Economist
- Fast Company
- Financial Times

Recommended Radio Shows and Podcasts
- BBC 4 Desert Island Discs
- Elizabeth Gilbert's 'Magic Lessons' Podcast

Recommended TV Shows or YouTube Videos
- TED Talks
- Shark Tank
- Dragon's Den
- The Apprentice
- Bloomberg Risk Takers
- Bloomberg Change Makers
- Planet of the Apps
- American Genius
- TechStars
- Grand Designs
- This Week in Startups
- Ramsay's Kitchen Nightmares
- How I Made My Millions
- Everything created by Charlie Brooker (such as How TV Ruined Your Life, Black Mirror)
- Mr. Selfridge (ITV's TV Drama)

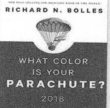

Are You Ready

for the

Next phase

of your ART JOURNEY?

THE SKY IS THE LIMIT!

ACKNOWLEDGEMENTS

The process of creating this book has been an act of passion and a labour of love that has seen the support of many people.

It has first and foremost been made possible by my beloved wife Sertac Sehlikoglu, my business partner Emre Haliloglu, my designer Murat Simsek, my project team members and friends Esat Artug and Abdulkadir Pir. I would like to thank my parents, my family members including Fatih Karakas and Merve Karakas, and my lovely students, friends, and colleagues at University of East Anglia, University of Cambridge PKP Summer School, McGill University, and Mountbatten Institute in London; who have continuously supported and inspired me during the process of creation. Special thanks go to UEA Enterprise Centre, Jon Carter, and Kevan Williams; Prof. Fiona Lettice, Robert Jones, and Louise Cutting at University of East Anglia. I owe a debt of gratitude to them for their enormous support, time, and help. They have believed in the potential of my ideas and constantly inspired me to pursue them. Without their encouragement and support, I would never have been able to create these doodles or finish this project. To them I offer deepest thanks for their gracious support and continuous enthusiasm for my work. In addition, I am deeply inspired by the books of Prof Adam Grant, Julia Cameron, Elizabeth Gilbert, and Chris Guillebeau.

My colleagues and friends all over the world have provided their morale and support to this project including Prof. Emine Sarigollu and Metin Ali Keles (Canada), Warren Nilsson and Tana Paddock (South Africa), Ismail Golgeci (Denmark), Eleni Tzouramani (United Arab Emirates), Rasim Coskun (United States), Femke Van Der Veer (Netherlands), Hayat Kabasakal and Muzaffer Bodur (Turkey), Jonathan Wilson, Ieva Martinaityte, Ratula Chakraborty, Paul Dobson, Graham Manville, Ana Sanz Vergel, Zografia Bika, Nikolaos Korfiatis and other NBS colleagues (UK). They have offered me wonderful help, feedback, guidance, and suggestions throughout this journey.

I remain grateful for our journey together. Thank you for walking this road with me.

Fahri Karakas

How You Can Use This Toolkit

- Get yourself prepared for the job market or a new career path
- Increase your confidence by exploring and building on your strengths
- Find out what brings out your excitement, curiosity, and enthusiasm
- Experiment with a diverse set of reflective, creative, and visual exercises to
- increase your professional skills, productivity, and happiness
- Learn the tools to design your life and career
- Imagine playful and fresh possibilities that will enlighten and inspire you
- Engage in a profound journey of self-exploration and unleash your best self
- Discover a powerful methodology to increase your learning and creativity

Made in the USA
Coppell, TX
19 September 2020